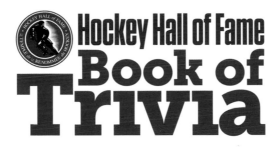

Hockey Hall of Fame
Book of
Trivia

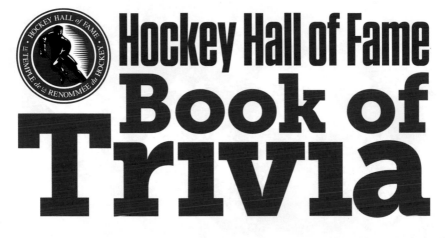

Hockey Hall of Fame
Book of
Trivia

Questions and Answers by Don Weekes

NHL CENTENNIAL EDITION
REVISED AND UPDATED

FIREFLY BOOKS

A FIREFLY BOOK

Published by Firefly Books Ltd. 2017
Copyright © 2017 Firefly Books Ltd.
Text copyright © 2017 Don Weekes

First printing

Publisher Cataloging-in-Publication Data (U.S.)
Title: Hockey Hall of Fame Book of Trivia : Questions and Answers / by Don Weekes.
Description: Richmond Hill, Ontario, Canada : Firefly Books, 2017. | NHL Centennial Edition |
    Includes bibliographic references and index. | Summary: "Hockey trivia book about the most
    celebrated and influential men and women who ever played hockey, including a new chapter
    celebrating the NHL centenary"—Provided by publisher.
Identifiers: ISBN 978-1-77085-954-8 (paperback)
Subjects: LCSH: Hockey—Biography. | Hockey Hall of Fame. | Hockey— Miscellanea.
Classification: LCC GV848.5A1W445 |
DDC 796.9620922 – dc23

Library and Archives Canada Cataloguing in Publication
Weekes, Don, author
    Hockey Hall of Fame book of trivia / questions and answers by Don Weekes.
—NHL centennial edition, revised and updated.

Includes index.
Includes bibliographical references and index.
ISBN 978-1-77085-954-8 (softcover)

    1. Hockey—Miscellanea. 2. National Hockey League—Miscellanea.
I. Title. II. Title: Book of trivia.

GV847.W38 2017 796.962'6402 C2017-902238-5

Published in the United States by
Firefly Books (U.S.) Inc.
P.O. Box 1338, Ellicott Station
Buffalo, New York 14205

Published in Canada by
Firefly Books Ltd.
50 Staples Avenue, Unit 1
Richmond Hill, Ontario L4B 0A7

Cover and interior design:
Gareth Lind, LINDdesign

Printed in China

Canada

*We acknowledge the financial support of the
Government of Canada.*

....

Photo Credits

Unless otherwise specified, all photos are
© Hockey Hall of Fame

Hockey Hall of Fame photographers and
collections represented: Steve Babineau, Paul
Bereswill, Studio Alain Brouillard, Michael Burns
Sr., Craig Campbell, Graphic Artists, Imperial
Oil—Turofsky, Fred Keenan, David Klutho,
Doug MacLellan, Matthew Manor, Mecca, Miles
Nadal, O-Pee-Chee, Portnoy, Frank Prazak,
Chris Relke, James Rice, Andre Ringuette, Dave
Sandford, Le Studio du Hockey and Jeff Vinnick.

© AP Images, 187, 190; © CP Images, 191; © CP
Images/Dave Buston, 224; © Icon Sportswire/
Scott W. Grau, 10; © Icon Sportswire/David
Hahn, 42; © Icon Sportswire/Michael Tureski, 42;
© Freestyle Photography/OSHC, 17; © Reuters/
Mario Anzuoni, 78; © Reuters/Mike Cassese, 78,
81; © Reuters/Greg Locke, 78; © Reuters/Mike
Segar, 78; © G.G. Bain/Shorpy Inc., 122.

Special thanks to the Bobby Orr Hall of Fame
in Parry Sound, Ontario, for the image of the
museum, 119.

Contents

HHOF Fan Forum

A Prize Beyond Reality

When Wayne Gretzky was inducted in 1999, he asked the Hall to create an event where fans could interact with him during his induction weekend. That idea started the Fan Forum, a tradition where honored players could share stories and memories and trade jabs with each other and those in attendance.

This second edition of the Hall's *Book of Trivia* has a touch of that laidback informality in its interactive approach, with questions that will make you wonder and answers that are bound to surprise even the most impassioned fan. Keeping it real, we also tried to dial back lionizing the game too much and stick to the raw details of what really went down. It's something not easily accomplished when glory is often the story.

Our hockey trivia from the first edition gets a refresh here. We've updated our last work, tweaking facts with new numbers to remain current and, in a few cases, bringing to light some fascinating details on freshly minted inductees. We also added a Chris Pronger-sized anniversary chapter to celebrate the mythmaking narratives throughout 100 years of NHL hockey. Like the man himself and his impact on team performance, we hope these new pages advance our entire Q&A to better reflect the Hall's collection of Player and Builder achievements.

To be honest, we kind of played with a short bench last time around, icing all the Hall greats we could cram into eight chapters and games—but still falling short as several big names went underrepresented with merely a mention. While more than 130 Hall of Famers were featured, inexcusably there was no story about Mark Messier. Or an exploit that defined the great Dominik Hasek. Or one that spoke of the

Joe Sakic

frustrations of three-time coach of the year Pat Burns.

So our reboot picks up where we left off in 2014—making up for any roster deficiencies with a full roar of talent current to this season's Hall Class. We fill those gaps and go deeper into the performances and personalities of Hall members. But our lineup still has holes. We had the nice problem of too many stories to tell in too few pages again.

Our second edition reminds me of something NHL stats guru Benny Ercolani recently said: "NHL numbers are only correct until the first game of the season." Then, everything changes, as players and teams pick up points, game by game. Thankfully, our numbers have a longer shelf life because player stats of Hall members are permanently established.

But Ercolani makes an important point, because every induction year there are new Hall members with new stories that shed light not only on their skills but, often, on the rarified play of past Hall greats: Who won the Hart Trophy MVP with the lowest point total? Which Hall of Famer joined her brother in a pro hockey game? And how many members of Detroit's Russian Five are Hall inductees?

A few old-timers finally got their due, too, like Lady Byng's first gentlemanly winner from a blue line corps, and the oldest NHL rookie ever. We didn't forget the future, opening the door to the Hall's waiting room with queries on the longshots and locks seeking immortality.

Without question, the early ambitions of all these players were typically modest. As we pointed out before, when Joe Sakic was inducted in 2012, he identified with the many who are "just hoping to play one game" in the NHL. His superstar career far surpassed his one-game target, but it was never so big that Sakic imagined his place in history among a pantheon of ice icons.

That's what makes their journey from ordinary to extraordinary to the Hall of Fame so special. It's a prize just beyond reality. No one is automatically bound for glory—even for those who stand above the rest. There is too much unknown out there to muck it up.

Welcome to our second edition. A comeback, of sorts. And who doesn't like a comeback starring the home team? Stay sharp.

— Don Weekes, May 2017

Alex Ovechkin

"If Not Today, Tomorrow"

Two days before Sergei Fedorov was inducted into the Hall of Fame in November 2015, Alex Ovechkin tallied goal 483 to tie his fellow Russian on their country's all-time NHL goal-scoring list. Ovechkin equalled it in 476 fewer games, but he couldn't break the mark when Washington met Fedorov's former team in Detroit three nights later. Ovechkin wanted it badly, firing a personal-best 15 shots on Red Wings goalie Petr Mrazek, though without success. Still, he remained upbeat: "If not today, tomorrow." His record-breaking 484th came five games later against Ottawa. By mid-January the Great 8 had become the first Russian to score 500 goals. In this chapter, we celebrate the NHL's centennial, from future Hall candidates like Ovechkin to hardnosed old-timer inductees with hockey names like Quackenbush and Waghorne.

1 Who scored the most power-play goals in a rookie season?

A. Teemu Selanne
of the Winnipeg Jets

B. Joe Nieuwendyk
of the Calgary Flames

C. Mike Bossy
of the New York Islanders

D. Alex Ovechkin
of the Washington Capitals

2 Which Hall member became the first French player drafted under new NHL rules in 1970 that denied the Montreal Canadiens first option on Quebec players?

A. Marcel Dionne of Drummondville

B. Réjean Houle of Rouyn

C. Gilbert Perreault of Victoriaville

D. Guy Lafleur of Thurso

3 Which NHL achievement(s) did Mike Modano realize during his Hall of Fame career?

A. Most goals by an American-born player

B. Most points by an American-born player

C. Most points and power-play points in the playoffs by an American-born player

D. All of the above

4 Who is Keila Penner?

A. A member of the Chicago Blackhawks' Ice Crew

B. An Ottawa fan whose school refused to let her wear her Senators jersey

C. An Edmonton teen whose Twitter post angered NHL boss Gary Bettman

D. An anthem singer who slipped on the ice after flubbing "The Star-Spangled Banner"

Answers 1-2

1 B. Joe Nieuwendyk of the Calgary Flames

A rookie on the power play is like letting a kid loose in a candy store—it could get messy. There are exceptions, such as Joe Nieuwendyk in 1987–88, when the All-American center from Cornell University tore up the NHL. Seldom has any team given so much responsibility to a player so early in his career, especially to one like Nieuwendyk, whose path to pro hockey was no cakewalk. He was never drafted into the OHL and was passed over entirely in his first year of NHL eligibility. When he finally went 27th overall in 1985 (his draft position came in a trade for Flames favorite Kent Nilsson), the *Calgary Herald* couldn't resist, famously headlining "Joe Who?" But Joe quickly proved to be a finisher. The kid could play down low, make accurate tip-ins and use his long reach in the crease. His mix of skills added a new dimension to the Flames' attack, particularly in critical situations on special teams. He netted an NHL-rookie record 31 power-play goals—just three off Tim Kerr's all-time mark of 34 goals. How sweet Joe was for Calgary.

Joe Nieuwendyk

Kids in the Candy Store: Top NHL Power-Play Rookies

Player	Induction Year	Team	Season	Total Goals	EV	PP	SH	GW
Joe Nieuwendyk	2011	Calgary	1987–88	51	17	31	3	8
Mike Bossy	1991	NY Islanders	1977–78	53	28	25	0	5
Teemu Selanne	Eligible in 2017	Winnipeg	1992–93	76	52	24	0	7
Alex Ovechkin	Active	Washington	2005–06	52	28	21	3	5
Rick Martin	Eligible	Buffalo	1971–72	44	25	19	0	5

2 C. Gilbert Perreault of Victoriaville

The Canadiens built their storied championships on secur-
ing the best talent available. While many believe they held
territorial rights to Quebec's top two players annually—and
that this is why they won so many Stanley Cups—it's just
not true. Montreal beat the bushes for prospects, like
every other team, and assigned them to a farm system
that existed until the amateur draft of the 1960s. The Habs,
however, did get an NHL rider that granted them priority
rights to two unsigned Quebec players, which may explain
the myth, though none proved NHL-caliber. In 1969, when
all amateurs became eligible for the draft, the league gave
Montreal the top two picks to end this "French rule." The
next year the consensus No. 1 was junior phenom Gilbert
Perreault. When expansion Buffalo won top choice, it was
a fait accompli, proving Bernie Geoffrion's assessment of
Perreault: "You could start a franchise with him." His was a
rare natural gift of pinball speed, slick stick work and skill
goals. Referee Frank Udvari said, "I've never seen a player
deke so many players out of their underwear." During
his 17-year career, Perreault was often overshadowed by
Guy Lafleur and Marcel Dionne. They were better, but, to
Perreault's credit, not by much.

Les Trois Étoiles of Quebec

Player	Induction Year	Career	GP	Scoring	Shots/%
Gilbert Perreault	1990	1970–1987	1191	512-814-1326	3079/16.6
Guy Lafleur	1988	1971–1991	1126	560-793-1353	3521/15.9
Marcel Dionne	1992	1971–1989	1348	731-1040-1771	3851/14.3

3 D. All of the above

It's been said that Mike Modano's game defied sports science and transcended box scores. His virtuoso performances not only made those around him better, they helped grow the sport in America's Southwest. It was no easy task in 1993, leaving hockey-mad Minnesota for a non-traditional market like Dallas. Further, Modano had a high hockey IQ and a great stick, but the speedy skater with a sizzling shot needed to play a three-zone game to be truly dominant. Modano's defensive metamorphosis combined with his puck savvy and easygoing personality soon warmed Texans. He became the face of the game in the Lone Star State, the Troy Aikman of hockey, as teammate Darryl Sydor said, referencing the Cowboys' gridiron great. Simply, Modano made hockey relevant in a climate with few rinks and zero high school programs. Even without his gaudy scoring numbers, 1999 Stanley Cup and 2002 Olympic silver medal, Modano, for everything he did to establish the game, might have qualified as a Hall Builder. In American Wild West mythology, the drifter-hero was often a young gun searching for a fresh start. He rode into town with secrets and a moral code. In hockey's frontier of Texas, that guy was Modano.

Mike Modano: An American Triggerman*

Most Goals		Most Points	
Player	**Totals**	**Player**	**Totals**
Mike Modano	561	Mike Modano	1347
Keith Tkachuk	538	Phil Housley	1232
Most Playoff Points		Most Playoff Power-Play Goals	
Mike Modano	146	Mike Modano	24
Chris Chelios	144	Kevin Stevens	20

*Not including Brett Hull, a dual citizen born in Canada

4 B. An Ottawa fan whose school refused to let her wear her Senators jersey

When Maple Grove Elementary School in Montreal held Habs Day to kick off the 2013 playoffs, school officials never figured their little event's buzz would be brought to national attention. But that's what happens when you put adults in charge. Instead of permitting Keila Penner to wear her Senators sweater, the school told the Grade 5 student she contravened dress code. Keila, 11, could either put on her school uniform or don a Habs jersey that the gym teacher offered. "I told her [the teacher] if you have a problem with my shirt, please call my dad," said Keila. Her classmates dissed her too, saying, "The Senators suck and they are going to lose tonight." Keila's father, Cary, was dumbfounded by the school's ruling. "I think they missed an opportunity to teach a good lesson ... about bullying," he said. Schoolboard bigwigs insisted that the principal acted in the student's best interest. When Senators owner Eugene Melnyk heard the news, he limoed the entire Penner family to Ottawa to watch Game 4 of the series at Scotiabank Place, which the Canadiens lost 3–2. If the Hall of Fame had an honor roll for the ordinary fan, Keila would be on it. Totally.

Keila Penner

5 What was Rob Blake's plus-minus number from his Norris Trophy season with the Los Angeles Kings in 1997–98?

A. Plus-103

B. Plus-53

C. Plus-23

D. Minus-3

6 How often did Gordie Howe actually notch a Gordie Howe hat trick of a goal, an assist and a fight in one game?

A. Only twice

B. Between 10 and 20 times

C. Between 20 and 30 times

D. More than 30 times

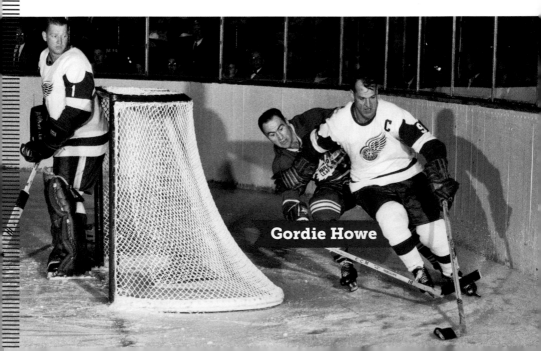

Gordie Howe

7 Among Hall of Fame goalies with at least 500 games played, who owns the NHL's best career save percentage since the league began tracking the stat in 1982–83?

A. Ed Belfour

B. Martin Brodeur

C. Dominik Hasek

D. Patrick Roy

8 Hall of Fame honoree Bill Quackenbush amassed how many penalties in 1948–49, when he became the first defenseman to win the Lady Byng Trophy?

A. No penalties: zero minutes

B. Less than 10 minors: under 20 minutes

C. Eleven to 20 minors: between 22 and 40 minutes

D. No Lady Byng winner has ever come from the blue line

Bill Quackenbush

5 D. Minus-3

Stranger things have happened. And this one even makes some hockey sense. Since the NHL began tracking plus-minus in 1967–68, three defensemen have won the James Norris Trophy sporting a minus. That means, in a half-century of Norris, three blue-liners have actually been judged the best all-around at their position despite allowing more goals-against than their own team scored with them on the ice at even strength. Did Norris voters simply neglect the subpar totals of Rob Blake (1997–98), Nicklas Lidstrom (2010–11) and Randy Carlyle (1980–81)? And what about the zero Rod Langway logged in his Norris-winning season of 1982–83? In all four cases, each man's Norris rivals had more-than-decent plus totals and twice led with higher point totals, such as in Blake's year. Blake, however, topped all blue-liners in goals, and his Kings, captained by No. 4, finished 20 points better than the previous season, the second-highest gain that year. All four men wore C's too, though Carlyle donned his the season following his award. These guys are blips on Norris' distinguished registry. But good blips. Because rewards come many ways. Numbers matter, but leadership counts.

Rob Blake

Rob Blake: A Measure of Norris Leadership in 1997–98

Player	Induction Year	Team Totals W–L–T	Scoring	+/−	Norris Votes
Rob Blake	2014	Los Angeles: 38-33-11	23-27-50	−3	401
Nicklas Lidstrom	2015	Detroit: 44-23-15	17-42-59	+22	369
Chris Pronger	2015	St. Louis: 45-29-8	9-27-36	+36	316

Gordie Howe

6 A. Only twice

Gordie Howe built his reputation as Mr. Hockey and Mr. Elbows on a nightly basis, settling scores with his stick for a point and his fists in a fight. Less deserving is his namesake's hat trick, which, while part of hockey's lexicon, was never really his, considering he neither introduced it nor set its unofficial record. In fact, through 26 NHL seasons, only two such tricks have been documented from Howe's 22 confirmed fights. The phrase is more tribute than fact, reflective of Howe's multi-skill set as a superstar who did everything other superstars could and some things they loathed, like fighting. Interestingly, both of Howe's tricks came at the Detroit Olympia in wins against Toronto during 1953–54. Howe registered one goal and two assists in each game, dueling with Fern Flaman in a battle of high sticks and punches in the first contest, and slicing Ted Kennedy's ear for eight stitches before they traded blows in the second. There is no firm consensus on a leader in this category, but nhl.com has Brendan Shanahan on top with 17.

A Misnomer: The Gordie Howe Hat Trick*

Date	Opposing Goalie	Goal Scorer on Assist	Opposing Fighter/ Team	Score
Oct. 11, 1953	Harry Lumley	Red Kelly	Fern Flaman	4-0 W
Mar. 21, 1954	Harry Lumley	Ted Lindsay	Ted Kennedy	6-1 W

*Some sources suggest Howe earned a third trick on October 26, 1967. However, his five-minute major was for high-sticking, not fighting.

7 C. Dominik Hasek

Dominik Hasek was an underdog's best friend. If he wasn't hauling the ordinary Buffalo Sabres on his back during their improbable 1999 Stanley Cup bid, then it was his Gumby-act heroics in the blue paint for the Czech Republic at the 1998 Olympics. The Sabres came within two wins of a championship, losing on Brett Hull's controversial overtime Cup-winner. A year earlier, his Czech squad, with only 11 NHLers—the fewest among top Olympic nations—captured gold for team and country. Hasek outdueled arch-nemesis Patrick Roy in a memorable winner-take-all shootout against Canada. His performance confirmed that goaltending is the most important position in the game, and Hasek its greatest practitioner. He won the prestigious Hart Trophy in 1997 and, in an NHL first for goalies, captured MVP honors again the following season, the first winner of consecutive seasons since Wayne Gretzky—with eye-popping save percentages of .930 and .932. But the little stories told more. Like in 1997–98, when he blanked 11 different teams in his 13-shutout campaign—the most clubs zeroed in a NHL season. The Dominator's lifetime save percentage? Over a 735-game career, a nimble .9223.

Bill Quackenbush

8 A. No penalties: zero minutes

As relationships go, there is no love lost between Lady Byng and defensemen. At best, it's a pretty rocky marriage, considering the task of stopping a phalanx of attacking puck carriers doesn't exactly encourage courteous play. While Byng voters did hand the sportsmanship prize to Brian Campbell in 2012, only two other rearguards have won the heart of Lady Byng in her 90-year history. Red Kelly earned three Byngs with Detroit in the early 1950s, and his mentor Bill Quackenbush one, in 1948–49.

"I wasn't a bodychecker," said Quackenbush. "I was a pokechecker. I found that if I did a lot of bodychecking, I got tired easily. I was on the ice an awful lot because I didn't get penalties." Quackenbush's rink management brought zero penalties that season, and he amassed only 95 minutes, including just one fighting major, throughout his entire 14-year career. He never checked to injure, instead maneuvering opponents off pucks before quarter-backing a rush up ice. Quackenbush was Lady Byng's first defenseman, and her last, among all winners, with zero penalty minutes.

9 Which Hall of Famer beat Bobby Hull as rookie of the year in 1957–58?

A.
Stan Mikita of the Chicago Black Hawks

B.
Frank Mahovlich of the Toronto Maple Leafs

C.
Gump Worsley of the New York Rangers

D.
Tim Horton of the Toronto Maple Leafs

10 Who owns the all-time record in Canada's three major junior leagues for most goals by a rookie in one season?

A. Don Murdoch with the WHL in 1974–75

B. Wayne Gretzky with the OHL in 1977–78

C. Pat LaFontaine with the QMJHL in 1982–83

D. Eric Lindros with the OHL in 1990–91

11

How long did it take Maurice Richard to break Nels Stewart's famous NHL career 324-goal record after Richard potted his first league goal?

A. Exactly 324 games

B. Exactly 500 points

C. Exactly 2,500 shots

D. Exactly 10 years

12

Before Patrick Roy accomplished it with Colorado in 2014, how many Hall of Famers won the Jack Adams Award as coach of the year with an NHL team they had played for?

A. Only one other individual: Pat Quinn

B. Two: Jacques Lemaire and Bill Barber

C. Three: Bob Pulford, Bill Barber and Pat Quinn

D. Four: Bob Pulford, Bill Barber, Pat Quinn and Lindy Ruff

Patrick Roy

9 B. Frank Mahovlich of the Toronto Maple Leafs

Hockey immortal Bobby Hull couldn't have lost the Calder Trophy to anyone better than Frank Mahovlich. By today's standards, their rookie showdown of 1957–58 might well be compared to the dueling pyrotechnics of Sidney Crosby and Alex Ovechkin in 2005–06. Both Hull and Mahovlich were natural talents and entered the league as teenagers bound for greatness. Hull stole the spotlight playing with the St. Catharines Teepees of the Ontario Hockey Association before signing with Chicago in 1957. Mahovlich put everyone on notice after landing MVP honors on 52 goals in 49 games with St. Michael's in Toronto. His smooth-skating, effortless style contrasted with Hull's powerful strides, but each man displayed an uncanny scoring knack, with masterful stickhandling and deadly accurate blasts. Their battle for top rookie was inevitable, and even though Hull's 13-34-47 out-pointed Mahovlich's, Calder voters were ultimately swayed by the Big M's 20-goal season. The balloting was close, among the tightest Calder races ever. Only four votes separated Mahovlich from Hull—a margin without match, even by the standards of Ovechkin-Crosby.

Frank Mahovlich

A Close Calder Call: Mahovlich Edges Out Hull

1957–58 Calder Trophy Balloting*					
Player	Age	Team	Votes	Vote%	Scoring
Frank Mahovlich	20	Toronto	120	37.15	20-16-36
Bobby Hull	19	Chicago	116	35.91	13-34-47
2005–06 Calder Trophy Balloting*					
Alex Ovechkin	20	Washington	1275	38.01	52-54-106
Sidney Crosby	18	Pittsburgh	831	24.78	39-63-102

*Calder Trophy voting is conducted by members of the Professional Hockey Writers Association. In 1957, Mahovlich received 82 first-place votes and 38 second-place votes, while Hull had 39 and 77, respectively. In 2006, individual voters ranked their top five candidates on a 10-7-5-3-1 points system. Ovechkin finished 124-5-0-0-0 and Crosby 4-95-19-10-1.

10 C. Pat LaFontaine with the QMJHL in 1982–83

They never knew what hit them. Storming the defense-challenged teams of the Quebec Major Junior Hockey League, Pat LaFontaine racked up a stupefying 104 goals as a rookie, a Canadian Hockey League mark that still stands. LaFontaine was born in St. Louis, Missouri, but was raised in suburban Detroit. Rather than opting for a U.S. college scholarship, he chose the less-likely path for American players, Canada's major junior system. LaFontaine joined the Verdun Juniors of the QMJHL, where sophomore Mario Lemieux played for rival Laval. Despite his first-year rank, LaFontaine crushed Lemieux's 84-100-184 count that season and league records of several prominent juniors, including Wayne Gretzky's rookie assist and point totals with Sault Ste. Marie. After eviscerating the CHL record books and bagging seven (yes, seven) league awards, there seemed little point in sticking around. LaFontaine's developmental arc was quantum—a third-overall pick in 1983 at 18 years old.

Rookie Junior Starts: Pat LaFontaine vs. The Greats

Player	Induction Year	Season	League	Scoring
Pat LaFontaine	2003	1982–83	QMJHL	104-130-234
Wayne Gretzky	1999	1977–78	OHL	70-112-182
Mario Lemieux	1997	1981–82	QMJHL	30-66-96

11 D. Exactly 10 years

Maurice Richard broke Nels Stewart's record of 324 goals on November 8, 1952—exactly 10 years to the date of his first NHL goal in 1942. During that decade Richard went from being a stubborn, brooding rookie with brittle bones—and occasional trade bait—to hockey deity, netting the league's first 50-goal season and lifting the Canadiens out of oblivion to two Stanley Cups. Sports reports from 1942 called Richard's first tally in the 10-4 shellacking of New York the "nicest goal of the tilt," a sensational end-to-end power drive reminiscent of Habs great Howie Morenz. Ten years to that day, the Rocket notched his 325th to become the NHL's all-time leading goal-scorer. The goal came like his first one—on a backhand—this time trickling through Chicago goalie Al Rollins. Flashbulbs popped and programs showered down on Richard, who collected the puck from the net and in an act of nervous tension produced sport's first spike (years before Homer Jones's first "touchdown spike" in 1965). He hurled it back to the ice, before gathering it up again. Ironically, Richard's famous puck is not in the Hall of Fame. It was sent to Her Majesty Queen Elizabeth at Buckingham Palace, where it is believed to still reside today.

Maurice Richard

12 C. Three: Bob Pulford, Bill Barber and Pat Quinn

Prior to Patrick Roy achieving it with the Avalanche, only Bob Pulford, Bill Barber and Pat Quinn had won the Jack Adams with one of their alma maters. Few individuals had Pulford's durability in the NHL. Through six decades he worked uninterrupted as a player, coach, general manager and executive. Because he was a cornerstone of Toronto's four Stanley Cups in the 1960s and, later, a longtime coach and executive in Chicago, few remember his Los Angeles years, two as a player followed by five as Kings coach. Pulford brought respectability to the young franchise, reversing years of poor defensive play with playoff berths beginning in 1974. He won the 1975 Adams after LA totaled 105 points, still a club record. Barber clicked on Philadelphia's famed LCB Line with Bobby Clarke and Reggie Leach during the 1970s. Among Philly's core of trigger-men, Barber "had the soul of a grinder but the talent of an artist," said beat reporter Jay Greenberg. His 2001 Adams came on a 31-13-7-3 record in 54 games after he took over as Flyers coach in December 2000, making him the first bench boss to win the Adams starting mid-season. Quinn was a player's player and a player's coach, twice winning the Adams, with Philadelphia in 1980 and Vancouver in 1992, where he had played 133 bruising games between 1970 and 1972.

Pat Quinn

29

13
When Mark Messier retired after more than 1,700 NHL games, how many fewer did he play than all-time leader Gordie Howe?

A. Only one game

B. The same total as his jersey number: 11

C. The same total as the difference between their career points: 37

D. The same total as the difference between their career goals: 107

14
How many players became Hall of Fame members while their pro contracts were still active?

A. According to Hall bylaws no player is eligible until retirement

B. Only one: Chris Pronger

C. Three: Gordie Howe, Guy Lafleur and Mario Lemieux

D. Four from the Toronto Maple Leafs

15 How old was Hall of Fame goalie Hugh Lehman when he made his NHL debut in 1926–27?

A. He was 17 years old

B. He was 29 years old

C. He was 36 years old

D. He was more than 40 years old

16 Only one NHLer registered a 200-goal career without having at least one 20-goal season. Who is that Hall member?

A.
Defenseman Larry Robinson

B.
Center Igor Larionov

C.
Left winger Bob Gainey

D.
Defenseman Scott Niedermayer

Mark Messier

13 B. The same total as his jersey number: 11

Character doesn't count for much in hockey without skill. Mark Messier had both in spades. After five Stanley Cups in Edmonton, Messier might be best remembered for his famous matter-of-fact prediction during the 1994 Eastern Conference Final with his Rangers on the brink of elimination: "We're going to go in and win Game 6." After guaranteeing New York fans a victory in New Jersey to stay alive and then delivering a third-period hat trick against the Devils' stifling neutral-zone trap, Messier proved he was the "Messiah," as so many fan signboards read. Later, in the memorable seven-game final against Vancouver, the Rangers' faithful reached their Promised Land on Messier's Cup winner, halting 54 years of denial. His quarter century of warrior hockey prematurely ended after watching the league cancel the 2004–05 season. In total, Moose played 1,756 games, just 11 shy of Gordie Howe's elusive 1,767 mark. Messier could have broken that all-time record with another season. But he didn't. Perhaps, he wanted to end his illustrious 25-year career that way—with a nod to Howe.

14 B. Only one: Chris Pronger

Chris Pronger filled many roles as a world-class athlete. The 6-foot-6 giant played both heavy and smart over 200 feet of ice. He could alter the course of a game without truce or mercy. Lethal hit, thunderous slapper, road grader tactics—they were all at his disposal. More roles soon followed. After his last game in November 2011, the oft-concussed. Pronger went on Philadelphia's injury reserve before taking a Flyers scouting job. Then, still under contract, and in the most startling of contradictions, Pronger, a serial offender with eight suspensions, started working for the NHL's Department of Player Safety, presumably because he recognizes better than most what's behind on-ice crimes. Understandably, on June 27, 2015, Philly unloaded him on Arizona for salary cap reasons. Forty-eight hours later, while technically an active player, he became a Class of 2015 nominee. This was possible because the Hall rewrote its eligibility bylaws months earlier, allowing injured players whose careers were over for three years to enter the Hall without obliging them to retire. That let Pronger earn the full amount of his seven-year, $34.9-million contract. Signed in 2010, he entered the Hall earning $525,000 per annum through to 2016-17. As a healthy Pronger said, "Nothing I have done has been the easy way, so I guess this follows suit."

Chris Pronger: Beast of the Blue Line

Regular Season 1993–2012					Playoffs 1996–2011				
GP	Scoring	+/−	PIM	Shots	GP	Scoring	+/−	PIM	Shots
1167	157-541-698	+183	1590	2610	173	26-95-121	+40	326	405

15 D. He was more than 40 years old

Hugh Lehman is one of hockey's truly forgotten innovators. His skating and stickhandling skills not only opened up the ice, but also the eyes of his peers who seldom dared venture beyond the posts. Lehman played a calculated-risk game that he rarely lost, chasing loose pucks down and head-manning them hard up ice to counterattack. His pioneering pokecheck startled onrushing forwards. On occasion Lehman even raced into the corners to engage opponents, becoming probably the game's first "third defenseman." "He was as valuable to his team as almost any two of his teammates," noted the *Winnipeg Free Press*. He accomplished all this before a roaming Jacques Plante revolutionized the position outside the crease and well before the trapezoid limited puck-passing netminders like Martin Brodeur. Lehman played most of his career on western clubs where he earned the nickname Old Eagle Eyes and won a Stanley Cup with the Vancouver Millionaires in 1915. He joined the NHL in 1926–27, when he was 41 years old, the oldest "rookie" in league history.

Hugh Lehman

16 A. Defenseman Larry Robinson

Analytics can't explain this aberration. Big Bird collected 208 career goals without having a single 20-goal season. In fact, among the NHL's top 25 goal-scoring defenseman, Larry Robinson is the sole rearguard lacking that standard. And like Bobby Orr and Scott Stevens, he never finished a season with a minus throughout an NHL career of 20-plus seasons. This defensively responsible approach is what distinguished Robinson's gamesmanship. His best years came as part of Montreal's Big Three, with Serge Savard and Guy Lapointe. The trio completely commanded the ice, balancing the Habs' offensive juggernaut with quickness and physical play in every zone. Robinson played a puck control and passing game, perhaps explaining why he never hit 20 goals, though he came agonizingly close twice, netting 19 in 1976–77 and 1985–86.

The Plus Side of Larry Robinson

Stat	NHL Achievement	Season(s)
20	Most consecutive plus seasons	1972–1992
+730	Highest plus-minus, career	1972–1992
+120	Second-highest plus-minus, one season	1976–77
133	Second-fewest shots by Norris Trophy winner	1979–80

17

Which Hall member famously threatened to retire during the 1960s rather than report to his traded team and then avoided league sanctions by signing with another club, the Toronto Maple Leafs?

A.	**B.**	**C.**	**D.**
Terry Sawchuk of the Detroit Red Wings	Andy Bathgate of the New York Rangers	Red Kelly of the Detroit Red Wings	Al Arbour of the Chicago Black Hawks

18

Which Hall of Famer joined her sibling as the first brother-sister tandem to play in a professional hockey game in North America?

A.	**B.**	**C.**	**D.**
Cammi Granato	Angela Ruggiero	Angela James	Geraldine Heaney

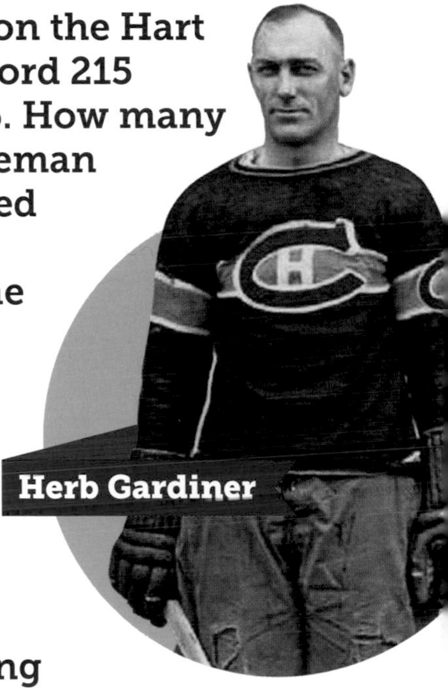

19 Wayne Gretzky won the Hart Trophy with a record 215 points in 1985–86. How many points did defenseman Herb Gardiner need to win his Hart in 1926–27's 36-game schedule?

A. 12 points

B. 24 points

C. 36 points

D. 72 points

Herb Gardiner

20 Despite never being a player, a coach, an official, an owner or an executive, he is a Hall member. Who enjoys this unique status?

A. Honorable Hartland Molson

B. Lord Stanley of Preston

C. Russian hockey czar Anatoli Tarasov

D. Monsignor Athol Murray

17 C. Red Kelly of the Detroit Red Wings

Red Kelly is the most accomplished player to successfully switch positions. His move from blue line to center came after his February 10, 1960, trade, one which landed the 12-year Detroit defenseman at center between wingers Frank Mahovlich and Bob Nevin on Toronto's top scoring line. Kelly's puck-carrying ability made for a smooth transition to offense, but the deal was mired in petty politics. How the Red Wings' loss became the Maple Leafs' gain in one of hockey's most lopsided deals began a week earlier after the *Detroit Free Press* reported new details about the previous spring's playoffs with the headline "Was Kelly Forced to Play on Broken Foot?" Two days later, a vengeful Jack Adams sent Kelly packing—to the New York Rangers. Kelly snubbed the last-place club and the next morning quit hockey. NHL president Clarence Campbell intervened, suggesting Kelly "think things over." Then, Toronto GM Punch Imlach came calling on Kelly, and the Simcoe, Ontario native was homeward bound as a Maple Leaf. Imlach gave up low-impact defenseman Marc Reaume, who played little after that except in minor pro circuits. In Toronto, Kelly's playmaking at center helped guide the Maple Leafs to four Stanley Cups.

Red Kelly

18 B. Angela Ruggiero

Angela Ruggiero always knew her life's goal. "I showed up to career day in the second grade with my hockey gear on," she said. "I knew I wanted to play hockey. I just didn't know where it would take me." That journey took "the girl" on boys' teams from her California home to Harvard, where she was an NCAA First-Team Academic All-American, then to four Olympics and 10 International Ice Hockey Federation Women's World Championships representing Team USA, and finally to the Hall of Fame as a Class of 2015 member. Ruggiero was named top defenseman numerous times in competition, and after 16 years on the national team program, no player had iced more games. "I like to be the intimidator," she said of her role as America's battle-hardened defender. Her physical presence brought more acclaim on January 28, 2005, when she and her brother, Bill, competed for the Central Hockey League's Tulsa Oilers, becoming the first brother and sister in a pro game in North America. Ruggiero was also the first female non-goalie on an NA pro squad. Hall member Cammi Granato recalled, "On the ice [Ruggiero] always played with the strength and edge that made her so dominant."

19 A. 12 points

Sport's greatest oxymoron might just be an MVP-worthy rookie. It has happened in hockey's modern era, but only to Wayne Gretzky. Prior to No. 99's Hart win as an NHL freshman in 1979–80, more than a half-century earlier, Nels Stewart was so venerated after his first season in 1925–26. A year later, Hart voters handed the prize to Herb Gardiner, who was a rookie by rule only at age 35, after years in the western pro loops. He took the Montreal Canadiens from the cellar to second overall in the 10-team league, and trimmed the Habs' goals against from 108 the previous season to a league-best 67 in 1926–27. That single-season turnaround proved Gardiner didn't need big stats for an MVP award. He managed an all-time Hart low of 12 points. Distilling down his feat gets tricky, but Gardiner, with the fewest points in Hart history, is the oldest MVP winner ever, despite being an NHL freshman. And Gretzky? He's the youngest Hart recipient at 19.5 years old.

20 B. Lord Stanley of Preston

Without ever playing any official role in the game, Lord Stanley could qualify as the only hockey fan elected to the Hall of Fame. Not unlike many enthusiasts, he immediately fell in love with the sport, witnessing his first match in his capacity as Canada's sixth governor-general at the Montreal Winter Carnival of 1889. Stanley's sons and daughter, Isobel, soon joined teams and played in exhibition contests on an outdoor rink made available by Stanley behind Rideau Hall in Ottawa. Ever an avid sports-man, in March 1892, Stanley donated a silver bowl to the "champion hockey team in the Dominion." Engraved with his family's coat of arms and crest, the Dominion Hockey Challenge Cup set Canada on a course that turned the country into a hockey nation, and his Cup into an icon of game supremacy. Stanley was a devoted fan, hockey parent and a sports patron of the highest order, but when he left Canada in 1893, he returned to his home country of England without ever seeing a match played for the trophy he established.

21 Who unseated Gordie Howe as the oldest player in NHL history to score a hat trick?

A.
Martin St-Louis of the
New York Rangers

B.
Teemu Selanne of the
Anaheim Ducks

C.
Jaromir Jagr of the
New Jersey Devils

D.
Mark Recchi of the Boston Bruins

22 Which NHL goalie did Hall of Fame inductee Cam Neely score most often against?

A. Patrick Roy, Class of 2006

C. Ed Belfour, Class of 2011

B. Mike Richter,
eligible since 2006

D. Dominik Hasek,
Class of 2014

23 Which defenseman holds the NHL record for most points in his rookie season?

A.
Ray Bourque of the Boston Bruins

B.
Gary Suter of the Calgary Flames

C.
Larry Murphy of the
Los Angeles Kings

D.
Brian Leetch of the
New York Rangers

24 Which Jack Adams Award winner was named the NHL's top coach most often during his Hall of Fame career?

A. Jacques Demers

B. Pat Burns

C. Pat Quinn

D. Scotty Bowman

21 C. Jaromir Jagr of the New Jersey Devils

Anytime someone breaks a Gordie Howe record, there's reason to celebrate. Just don't remind Jaromir Jagr. He happily scored three times against Philadelphia in January 2015, but was not too thrilled about topping Howe's age mark. "I like to score hat trick, but...I don't want to be the oldest guy," said Jagr, who eclipsed Mr. Hockey by more than a year. In his prime, Jagr's offensive dazzle combined athletic artistry and clutch timing, earning him frequent praise as a human highlight reel. After two Stanley Cups in 11 seasons with Pittsburgh, he became a free-agent mercenary, playing for another eight clubs, including three years with Omsk in the Kontinental Hockey League. His record-setting 15th hat trick came just shy of his 43rd birthday, against the Flyers' Ray Emery and backup Steve Mason in a 5–2 New Jersey win. His scoring touch diminshed, Jagr found new life with Florida in 2015–16, scoring 66 points thanks to his Cheliosian genes and linemates half his age. He even hinted that he would play until 50, a sign of his growing acceptance as hockey's eldest skatesman.

Reigning Hats: The NHL's Oldest Trick Turners

Player	Team	Date	Score	Opponent	Career HT No.	Age
Jaromir Jagr	New Jersey	Jan. 3, 2015	5–2 W	Philadelphia	15th	42.1
Gordie Howe	Detroit	Nov. 2, 1969	4–3 W	Pittsburgh	19th	41.7
Teemu Selanne	Anaheim	Mar. 28, 2011	5–4 W	Colorado	22nd	40.8

22 A. Patrick Roy, Class of 2006

Cam Neely had a way of terrorizing goalies that made him the premier power forward of his generation. Few defensemen could slow him on the attack or outmuscle him along the walls. Once across the blue line, Neely's scoring instincts and quick release took over. He netted 452 career goals, 34 of them against Patrick Roy, his favorite target. "In regards to Patrick, I really understood the way he played," Neely told the *Montreal Gazette*. "There were only a couple places to put the puck on him without taking the time to look—the top corner (as Roy did the butterfly) or between the legs as he was going down." Neely's dominance over hockey's second-winningest netminder included 16 regular-season goals and 18 playoff markers, two of them during the 1988 Adams Division Final, which awarded the Bruins their first series victory over Montreal after 18 straight postseason losses. According to hockeyfights.com Neely had 79 career fights, but the final blow was a knee from Ulf Samuelsson during the 1991 playoffs that effectively ended his career. Neely also beat Roy another way, being inducted the year before him, in 2005.

Cam Neely: The Archetypal Power Forward

Regular Season 1983–1996					Playoffs 1984–1995				
GP	Scoring	+/−	PIM	Shots	GP	Scoring	+/−	PIM	Shots
726	395-299-694	+82	1241	2148	93	57-32-89	−9	168	291

Cam Neely

23 C. Larry Murphy of the Los Angeles Kings

Surprised? Larry Murphy might be the quietest record holder of a major league mark. Never as conspicuous as offense-minded rearguards like Ray Bourque or Brian Leetch, Murphy went about his trade with quiet efficiency, working hard defensively and directing attacks, while producing points of an unspectacular variety. His two-way game, however, revealed his hockey smarts. He read the ice well and practiced an intelligent shot selection, choosing a low wrister over a big slap for better accuracy. On the blue line, Murphy played the puck more than the man, which explains his low penalty count, averaging about 50 minutes per season through 21 years. Underrated? Absolutely. Without an individual award to call his own, he's a 1,000-point defender who won four Stanley Cups. His show-off year might be 1980–81. Kings coach Bob Berry gave his wunderkind rookie veteran minutes and Murphy responded, though at times he played more like a forward who occasionally skated backward to protect his net, as some said. His NHL-record 76 points that season foretold his future, with lots of scoring but little individual hardware, as he played bridesmaid in Calder Trophy voting to Peter Stastny.

The NHL's All-Time Top Scoring Rookie Defensemen

Player	Induction Year	Team	Season	GP	Scoring
Larry Murphy	2004	Los Angeles	1980–81	80	16-60-76
Brian Leetch	2009	NY Rangers	1988–89	68	23-48-71
Gary Suter	Eligible	Calgary	1985–86	80	18-50-68
Phil Housley	2015	Buffalo	1982–83	77	19-47-66
Ray Bourque	2004	Boston	1979–80	80	17-48-65

24 B. Pat Burns

Pat Burns may be the best example of hockey's familiar hired-to-be-fired theory of NHL coaching. His three Jack Adams Awards contributed little to his own success and proved coach-of-the-year is one step from a pink slip, which he received after awards in his first seasons with Montreal, Toronto and Boston. Ironically, Burns was named top coach everywhere except New Jersey, his only championship club. But this isn't surprising. Only three bench bosses earned an Adams following a Stanley Cup. No one had coached more playoff games (120) before winning the Cup and with more NHL teams (4) than Burns. He was intimidating and a brute behind the bench, but he was also fair and possessed a warm, humorous side. One thousand well-wishers attended his funeral in November 2010, a measure of the man who once said of the tenuous career path, "I don't want to be coach of the year. I only want to be coach for a year."

Pat Burns: A Trophy Case of Adams (Plus a Stanley)

Season	Team	Award	GC	Record	Points	Division Finish
1988–89	Montreal	Jack Adams	80	53-18-9	115	1st
1992–93	Toronto	Jack Adams	84	44-29-11	99	3rd
1997–98	Boston	Jack Adams	82	39-30-13	91	2nd
2002–03*	New Jersey	Stanley Cup	82	46-20-10-6	108	1st

*Burns won the Cup with a 16-8 record in the playoffs.

25 The Conn Smythe Trophy was donated by Maple Leaf Gardens in 1964 to honor the Toronto coach, manager, owner and founder. Awarded annually to the NHL's playoff MVP, how many Maple Leafs have actually won it?

A.
Only one: Dave Keon

B.
Two: George Armstrong and Johnny Bower

C.
Three: Dave Keon, George Armstrong and Johnny Bower

D.
No Maple Leaf player has won the Conn Smythe

26 Prior to Sidney Crosby and Evgeni Malkin doing it with Pittsburgh in 2006–07, which Hall of Famers were the last teammates to win the NHL scoring and rookie scoring races in the same season?

A. Bobby Hull and Bill Hay with the Chicago Black Hawks

B. Bryan Trottier and Mike Bossy with the New York Islanders

C. Mario Lemieux and Jaromir Jagr with the Pittsburgh Penguins

D. It never happened before Crosby and Malkin

27 Who logged the most NHL seasons to equal Gordie Howe's league record?

A.
Mark Messier

B.
Tim Horton

C.
Alex Delvecchio

D.
Chris Chelios

28 What was Lanny McDonald referring to when he said, "This is the most peaceful feeling in hockey"?

A. His assist on teammate Darryl Sittler's 1976 Canada Cup-winner

B. His acrimonious departure from Harold Ballard's Maple Leafs in 1979

C. His Stanley Cup championship in 1989

D. His 1992 entry into the Hall of Fame

Lanny McDonald

25 A. Only one: Dave Keon

There's real irony in Toronto sponsoring an MVP award for Stanley Cup playoff excellence. The club, riding a 50-year Cup drought, hasn't exactly oozed championship jelly. The Gardens presented the Conn Smythe after the Leafs' dynasty of the early 1960s. At the time, optimism reigned at Carlton and Church, and a new MVP award honoring Smythe seemed appropriate. Jean Béliveau won it initially in 1965 and Roger Crozier next, followed by Dave Keon playing on coach Punch Imlach's Over-The-Hill Gang of 1967. But since then? Well, the hockey gods have a wicked sense of humor. Keon remains Smythe's lone Leafs representative. He hit the ice hard every shift, a relentless two-way dynamo with speed to burn and a compete level to match. Neither big nor tough, he killed penalties and rarely took any, leading all 1,000-game players with just 117 career minutes through 18 seasons. Or about the average box time many NHLers accrue seasonally. Keon has been called the ideal player—even with his undersized frame. Durable, devoted and not just respected, he was popular. Then it all went sideways after a spiteful Harold Ballard failed to sign him in 1975. Keon left Toronto bitter, and he remained largely a Leafs alumnus in absentia until their centennial season of 2016–17, when the club made amends and named him their greatest all-time player.

Bill Hay

Bobby Hull

26 A. Bobby Hull and Bill Hay with the Chicago Black Hawks

Few NHL teams have iced rosters with duo scoring leaders. Before Crosby and Malkin turned the trick, it hadn't happened since 1959–60 when Bobby Hull won the points title and linemate Bill Hay led all rookies. Hull's prime years as hockey's Golden Jet were just taking off. All season, the 21-year-old battled Boston's Bronco Horvath in an Art Ross race that was decided by Hull's one assist in the season's final game. His pivot was 24-year-old freshman Hay, who debuted as the first college player in the NHL but became more famous as Hull's setup man with Murray Balfour on the Million Dollar Line. The trio gelled almost overnight, playing large roles in each other's careers, including fast-tracking Hull's emergence as a superstar. "Bill was strong and could control the puck," said Hull. "Murray was a bulldog who fore-checked and back-checked. We just worked out fabulously well." Hay served as president of the Calgary Flames and, later, as president of Hockey Canada. He spent 33 years at the Hall, including as its chairman and CEO.

Bobby Hull and Bill Hay: The Hawks' Dynamic Duo of 1959–60

Scoring Race Leaders			Rookie Scoring Race Leaders		
Player	Team	Scoring	Player	Team	Scoring
Bobby Hull	Chicago	39-42-81	Bill Hay	Chicago	18-37-55
Bronco Horvath	Boston	39-41-80	Murray Oliver	Detroit	20-19-39

27 D. Chris Chelios

Greybeards own several inspiring yet unofficial NHL records. Johnny Bucyk is the oldest 50-goal scorer at 35. Dominik Hasek is the oldest goalie to hoist a Stanley Cup at 43. They're considered achievements without any formal recognition in league record books. However, among those endurance benchmarks that are credited, the most hallowed is Gordie Howe's 26 seasons played across an incomprehensible five different decades. His 30-year grip on the mark was finally pried open by ageless warhorse Chris Chelios during his last crusade in 2009–10. Both men were freaks of nature, born with exceptional genetics in near-indestructible bodies. Further, neither knew the word quit, especially while sparring with 20- and 30-year-olds. Howe's staying power was cyborg-like, playing until he was 52. Chelios' durability was grounded in a sick strengthening regime of mountain biking, paddleboarding and riding a stationary bike in a sauna. When asked if he ever thought about his old age, Chelios said, "Only every time I think about Gordie Howe."

Chris Chelios: A Spartan at Heart

Most Seasons		Most Years in Playoffs	
Player	Totals	Player	Totals
Gordie Howe	26	Chris Chelios	24
Chris Chelios	26	Ray Bourque	21
Most Playoff Games		Most Teams with 400 Games Played	
Chris Chelios	266	Chris Chelios	3 (Montreal 402, Chicago 664, Detroit 578)
Nicklas Lidstrom	263		

28 C. His Stanley Cup championship in 1989

Lanny McDonald had an uncanny knack for reaching the ultimate prize in the nick of time. The career benchmark of 500 goals? McDonald sneaked into those prestigious ranks on his final goal, No. 500. The playmaker's standard of one thousand points? McDonald clawed out 1,006 points during 1,111 regular-season games. The Stanley Cup? It finally came as co-captain with Calgary in 1988–89, his last hurrah. It was a storybook season for the red-haired veteran with his trademark bushy mustache. In the Cup-clinching Game 6 against Montreal, McDonald again met his objective, scoring a crucial go-ahead goal, his lone marker of the 1989 play-offs. Realizing his elusive dream after a long chase brought final validation. "This is the most peaceful feeling in hockey. There's no feeling like it," said McDonald after hoisting Stanley. "I wish I could describe it to people outside. I think you appreciate it a lot more after you've been trying to win it for 16 years, like I have."

29 **What innovation is attributed to Hall of Famer Fred Waghorne?**

A. Pro hockey's first visor rule

B. Dropping the puck at faceoffs

C. Synthetic leg pads for goalies

D. Flexible goal pegs that anchor nets to the ice

30 **How often did Phil Housley win a major NHL trophy during his 21-year Hall of Fame career?**

A. Only once: the Norris Trophy as top defenseman

B. Three times: the Calder Trophy as top rookie and two Norris Trophies

C. Five times

D. Housley never won any NHL awards

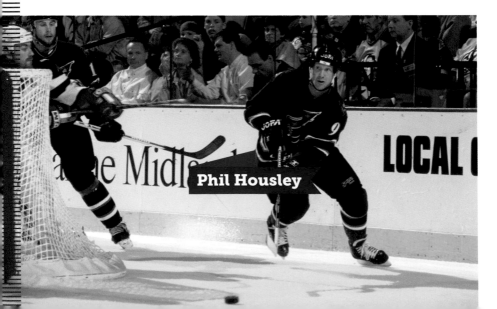

Phil Housley

31 Legendary broadcaster Danny Gallivan coined the expression "spin-o-rama" to describe a deke first used by which Hall of Famer?

A.
Serge Savard of the Montreal Canadiens

B.
Bobby Orr of the Boston Bruins

C.
Dave Keon of the Toronto Maple Leafs

D.
Denis Savard of the Chicago Blackhawks

32 Who is the oldest scoring champion in NHL history?

A.
Bill Cook of the New York Rangers in 1932–33

B.
Gordie Howe of the Detroit Red Wings in 1962–63

C.
Wayne Gretzky of the Los Angeles Kings in 1993–94

D.
Martin St-Louis of the Tampa Bay Lightning in 2012–13

Answers 29-30

29 B. Dropping the puck at faceoffs

He's largely unknown, but every time players faceoff today, it's thanks to Fred Waghorne. At one time, officials typically placed the puck between opposing centermen and shouted "Play" to initiate action. Waghorne changed that simply out of self-preservation after one too many stick whacks to his ankles and shins. Dropping the puck from a few feet above the ice allowed him time to back away, sidestepping the flurry of sticks for good. He also played a role in the use of the referee's whistle and cowbell. It's unclear what Waghorn's actual contributions were, some believe that he pioneered the whistle to replace the traditional cowbell to halt play; others suggest the opposite, that he replaced the whistle with the cowbell because fans used bells as noisemakers and metal whistles could freeze up—this all before plastic whistles became the standard play stopper. However, his greatest achievement may have come off-ice as a league organizer. Waghorne founded several Toronto-area loops, including the Beaches Hockey League in 1911, which evolved into the Metropolitan Toronto Hockey League, probably the largest minor hockey association in the world. While Waghorne gave hockey its most familiar game procedure and officiated some 1,700 games without fear or favor, his efforts as a league founder and administrator are what made this pioneer referee a Hall Builder.

30 D. Housley never won any NHL awards

Blessed with blazing speed and acceleration, Phil Housley was the complete finesse package. So wow was his raw talent that the high schooler transitioned straight into an NHL career and never looked back. He was anointed into elite company, including Bobby Orr's, who had 25 fewer points in his rookie start than Housley's 66 freshman total. By mid-career, Housley had become the fleet-footed points machine every team needed on the back end. Unlike Orr, however, the trophies awarded to honor his skill level eluded him. He faced stiff Norris rivals in Paul Coffey and Ray Bourque, each also outvoting him in First All-Star berths. His timing stank at Stanley Cups, too. Housley played in more games (1,495) than any NHLer without winning a Cup. The lack of shiny bobbles and a career plus-minus of minus-53 probably caused his nine-year Hall wait. As usual, someone always seemed more deserving. In 2015, Housley, the highest-scoring American-born player after Mike Modano, finally got his Hall due, in residence with the keepers of the greatest hockey awards in the world.

**Phil Housley:
A Star without
Silverware**

Career	GP	Scoring	+/–	PIM	Shots	Shots %
1982–2003	1495	338-894-1232	−53	822	3808	8.9

31 A. Serge Savard of the Montreal Canadiens

CBC's Danny Gallivan, the premier wordsmith in hockey, introduced many signature terms to today's play-by-play repertoire, including "spin-o-rama." While Bobby Orr and Denis Savard are more widely linked to that shifty, on-the-rush 360-degree swivel, Gallivan was first inspired by the deft swirling rotation of Serge Savard, who originated the action to evade attacking forwards during the late 1960s. Later, Denis Savard, perfected the same pivot. "It started off with me just turning my back to the defenseman to keep the puck away," said Denis. "Then, I thought about it and said, 'Hey, this could be a pretty good move." Gallivan's colorful delivery, voice and genuine enthusiasm made hockey more thrilling for fans. His phrasings, delivered as fast as the play developed and mixed with the game's lexicon, became his distinctive broadcast style. In 1984, Gallivan won the Hall's Foster Hewitt Memorial Award for his outstanding contribution to hockey broadcasting.

32 D. Martin St-Louis of the Tampa Bay Lightning in 2012–13

When Martin St-Louis joins the Hall of Fame sometime after 2018, much will be made of his unlikely rise to NHL stardom. Four inches shorter and 20 pounds lighter than the average player in the 1990s, St-Louis went undrafted and didn't play his first NHL game until he was 23, with Calgary. Two years and a free-agent signing later, he caught lightning in a bottle with Tampa Bay as the league's hardest-working right winger, collecting the Art Ross, Hart and Pearson Trophies and the Stanley Cup in 2004. During his second scoring championship in 2012–13, St-Louis defied the oracles again, this time becoming the oldest scoring leader in NHL history at 37 years old. It fell on the 80th anniversary of Bill Cook's historic title in 1932–33. Both men did it in 48-game schedules. Perhaps, that provided an advantage. Nevertheless, it proved both men could still play as older skaters and make a difference despite their age. And in St-Louis' case, a difference irrespective of his size or draft status. No one is ever too small, too old or too overlooked to win Art Ross' approval.

Fountain of Youth:
The NHL's Oldest Scoring Champions

Player	Team	Season	Scoring	GP	Age
1. Martin St-Louis	Tampa Bay	2012–13	17-43-60	48	37.1
2. Bill Cook	NY Rangers	1932–33	28-22-50	48	36.5
3. Gordie Howe	Detroit	1962–63	38-48-86	70	34.11
4. Newsy Lalonde	Montreal	1920–21	33-10-43	24	33.4
5. Wayne Gretzky	Los Angeles	1993–94	38-92-130	81	33.3

They Call Him Mr. Hockey

Future Hall of Famers are seldom saddled with nicknames such as Redlight (Andre Racicot) or Suitcase (Gary Smith) or the Rat (Ken Linseman). Hall honorees have been called Fats (Alex Delvecchio) and Apple Cheeks (Harry Lumley) during their playing days, but top NHL talents usually earn a handle that reflects their speed, size, agility, toughness or status among hockey's scoring elite. Some monikers even personified the player's position or team or even the game itself. In this game, check out the best hockey nicknames belonging to Hall members and contenders and match them to their rightful owner.

For solutions, turn the page.

Speed

1.	Golden Jet	A. Pavel Bure
2.	Russian Rocket	B. Bobby Hull
3.	Bullet Joe	C. Maurice Richard
4.	Le démon blond	D. Teemu Selanne
5.	Finnish Flash	E. Guy Lafleur
6.	Rocket	F. Joe Simpson

Size

1.	Big Bird	A. Mark Messier
2.	Moose	B. Jean Béliveau
3.	The Big M	C. Marcel Dionne
4.	Shrimp	D. Larry Robinson
5.	Little Beaver	E. Roy Worters
6.	Gros Bill	F. Frank Mahovlich

Agility

1.	Jake the Snake	A. Ed Belfour
2.	Thieving Giraffe	B. Yvan Cournoyer
3.	Roadrunner	C. Jacques Plante
4.	Dipsy-Doodle-Dandy	D. Ken Dryden
5.	Eddie the Eagle	E. Emile Francis
6.	The Cat	F. Max Bentley

Toughness

1.	Terrible Ted	A. Doug Gilmour
2.	Hatchet Man	B. Billy Smith
3.	Punch	C. Emile Bouchard
4.	Killer	D. Jack Stewart
5.	Butch	E. Harry Broadbent
6.	Black Jack	F. Ted Lindsay

Scoring

1.	Boom-Boom	A. Mario Lemieux
2.	Peter the Great	B. Nels Stewart
3.	The Big Bomber	C. Bernie Geoffrion
4.	Old Poison	D. Charlie Conacher
5.	The Babe Ruth of Hockey	E. Howie Morenz
6.	Super Mario	F. Peter Forsberg

Respectability

1.	Mr. Hockey	A. Dominik Hasek
2.	St. Patrick	B. Gordie Howe
3.	Dominator	C. Patrick Roy
4.	Mr. Goalie	D. Wayne Gretzky
5.	Ronnie Franchise	E. Glenn Hall
6.	The Great One	F. Ron Francis

They Call Him Mr. Hockey
Solutions

Speed
1. Golden Jet	**B. Bobby Hull**
2. Russian Rocket	**A. Pavel Bure**
3. Bullet Joe	**F. Joe Simpson**
4. Le démon blond	**E. Guy Lafleur**
5. Finnish Flash	**D. Teemu Selanne**
6. Rocket	**C. Maurice Richard**

Toughness
1. Terrible Ted	**F. Ted Lindsay**
2. Hatchet Man	**B. Billy Smith**
3. Punch	**E. Harry Broadbent**
4. Killer	**A. Doug Gilmour**
5. Butch	**C. Emile Bouchard**
6. Black Jack	**D. Jack Stewart**

Size
1. Big Bird	**D. Larry Robinson**
2. Moose	**A. Mark Messier**
3. The Big M	**F. Frank Mahovlich**
4. Shrimp	**E. Roy Worters**
5. Little Beaver	**C. Marcel Dionne**
6. Gros Bill	**B. Jean Béliveau**

Scoring
1. Boom-Boom	**C. Bernie Geoffrion**
2. Peter the Great	**F. Peter Forsberg**
3. The Big Bomber	**D. Charlie Conacher**
4. Old Poison	**B. Nels Stewart**
5. The Babe Ruth of Hockey	**E. Howie Morenz**
6. Super Mario	**A. Mario Lemieux**

Agility
1. Jake the Snake	**C. Jacques Plante**
2. Thieving Giraffe	**D. Ken Dryden**
3. Roadrunner	**B. Yvan Cournoyer**
4. Dipsy-Doodle-Dandy	**F. Max Bentley**
5. Eddie the Eagle	**A. Ed Belfour**
6. The Cat	**E. Emile Francis**

Respectability
1. Mr. Hockey	**B. Gordie Howe**
2. St. Patrick	**C. Patrick Roy**
3. Dominator	**A. Dominik Hasek**
4. Mr. Goalie	**E. Glenn Hall**
5. Ronnie Franchise	**F. Ron Francis**
6. The Great One	**D. Wayne Gretzky**

Ronnie Franchise

Luc Robitaille

No Ordinary Path

There is no singular achievement in hockey greater than being honored in the Hockey Hall of Fame. At his 2009 induction ceremony, Luc Robitaille admitted that he never set out to be recognized alongside stars such as Wayne Gretzky, Maurice Richard or Guy Lafleur: "I just wanted to play in the NHL, and to have this happen, it's something truly amazing." The 171st draft pick of 1984, Robitaille spoke of hope for kids of all abilities: "Be a light; follow your dreams. Anything is possible!" In this opening chapter, we humbly present the extraordinary paths some individuals took to the Hall.

33 Which Hall of Fame member gave hockey the expression, "He shoots! He scores!"?

A. An NHL player

B. A broadcaster

C. A seven-year-old stick boy

D. A spectator

34 Who is the youngest player to be inducted into the Hall of Fame?

A.	B.	C.	D.
Bobby Orr	Ken Dryden	Vladislav Tretiak	Mario Lemieux

35 How many players became Hall of Famers without the normal three-year waiting period between retirement and induction?

A. Only three players

B. Five players

C. 10 players

D. 20 players

 Who was inducted into the Hall of Fame at the same time as goalie great Jacques Plante, in 1978?

A. The NHL coach who demoted Plante to the minors

B. The NHL general manager who traded Plante twice

C. A goalie who beat out Plante for the Vezina Trophy

D. The shooter responsible for forcing Plante to wear his famous mask

A broadcaster

Foster Hewitt was the voice of hockey for more than half a century and the author of its most familiar phrase, "He shoots! He scores!" In a distinctive shrill warble from his famous gondola at Maple Leaf Gardens, Hewitt called thousands of matches first on radio and later on television, becoming the mind's eye for two generations of sports fans, not only in Canada but around the world. For his contribution to the growth and development of the game during a length of service unrivaled by his peers, Hewitt was inducted into the Builder category in the Hall of Fame in 1965, the only broadcaster so honored.

Foster Hewitt

34 A. Bobby Orr

When Bobby Orr and Mario Lemieux entered the Hall of Fame, they were years younger than their fellow inductees thanks to two factors: both stars suffered serious health issues mid-career, and both deked the Hall's customary three-year wait for eligibility. Each was recognized in his retirement year: Orr in 1979 and Lemieux after his first farewell, in 1997. Orr was just 31 years old, his extraordinary career having been cut short by bad knees. Lemieux makes this answer a squeaker—at 32, he was just a year older than Orr. Dryden is the youngest goalie to be inducted into the Hall, at age 36. Orr's induction was bittersweet; as he said, "The only thing that could top this would be to be back on the ice as a player."

The Youngest Hall of Famers

Player	Induction Year	Date of Birth	Age When Inducted
Bobby Orr	1979	March 20, 1948	31.6 years
Mario Lemieux	1997	October 5, 1965	32.2 years
Mike Bossy	1991	January 22, 1957	34.8 years
Ken Dryden	1983	August 8, 1947	36.1 years
Guy Lafleur	1988	September 20, 1951	36.11 years
Vladislav Tretiak	1989	April 25, 1952	37.6 years
Bobby Clarke	1987	August 13, 1949	37.1 years

35 C. 10 players

These 10 guys are the All-Star Team of the Hall of Fame. Playing in net on this ultimate fantasy squad is Terry Sawchuk, with defensive partners Dit Clapper and Bobby Orr on the blue line. Up front are two superstar lines: one is centered by Jean Béliveau with wingmen Gordie Howe and Ted Lindsay, and the second trio is led by Wayne Gretzky, centering Mario Lemieux and Maurice Richard. The multi-purpose Red Kelly fills in as a spare forward or defenseman. This roster might be set for a while. Following Gretzky's 1999 farewell, the Hall's board of governors decided that all players must be retired three years before nomination, except under certain humanitarian circumstances.

The Honor Role of Immediate Hall Inductees

Player	Induction Year	GP	Selected Honors
Dit Clapper	1947	833	1st All-Star (3)
Maurice Richard	1961	978	Hart (1), 1st All-Star (8)
Ted Lindsay	1966	1068	Art Ross (1), 1st All-Star (8)
Red Kelly	1969	1316	Norris (1), Lady Byng (4), 1st All-Star (6)
Terry Sawchuk	1971	971	Calder (1), Vezina (4), 1st All-Star (3)
Jean Béliveau	1972	1125	Art Ross (1), Hart (2), 1st All-Star (6), Conn Smythe (1)
Gordie Howe	1972	1767	Art Ross (6), Hart (6), 1st All-Star (12)
Bobby Orr	1979	657	Calder (1), Norris (8), Art Ross (2), Hart (3), 1st All-Star (8), Conn Smythe (2)
Mario Lemieux	1997	915	Calder (1), Art Ross (6), Hart (3), 1st All-Star (5), Conn Smythe (2)
Wayne Gretzky	1999	1487	Art Ross (10), Hart (9), Lady Byng (5), 1st All-Star (8), Conn Smythe (2)

36 D. The shooter responsible for forcing Plante to wear his famous mask

Few hockey fans missed the irony of Jacques Plante and Andy Bathgate's Hall of Fame inductions in 1978. It was Bathgate who, on November 1, 1959, whipped a backhander that split Plante's nose, forcing the Canadiens netminder to the clinic for stitchwork. Despite coach Toe Blake's objections, Plante returned to the ice armed with his practice mask—a primitive fiberglass protector with holes for the eyes and mouth. He would wear one the rest of his career, forever changing the game by introducing what would become the most important piece of equipment in a goaltender's arsenal. Bathgate admitted his fateful blast was deliberately aimed flush at the Canadiens goalie's face, as payback after Plante had leveled him earlier in the match. Bathgate's devastating slapper could also hurt an entire team: the previous season (1958–59), he had scored 40 goals and won the Hart Trophy as league MVP. Later, he tied Bobby Hull as NHL scoring leader and claimed his only Stanley Cup after a trade to Toronto in 1964. Both men retired in 1975 after playing for WHA teams, Plante in Edmonton and Bathgate in Vancouver.

Andy Bathgate

37 Which NHLer didn't attend his Hall of Fame ceremony because his wife wasn't welcome at the event?

A.
Eddie Shore

B.
Ted Lindsay

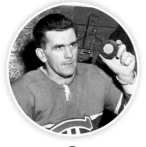

C.
Maurice Richard

D.
George Armstrong

38 Several players from hockey's seven-man era are immortalized in the Hall for their play as the team's seventh man on the ice. What was that position?

A.	**B.**	**C.**	**D.**
The rover	The half-center	The mid-guard	The quarter slot

39 How many NHL scoring lines have all three members in the Hall of Fame?

A.
Only two lines

B.
Four lines

C.
Seven lines

D.
10 or more lines

40 Which NHLer retired with the most career points by an undrafted player and went on to become a Hall of Fame member?

A.
Joe Mullen

B.
Peter Stastny

C.
Adam Oates

D.
Borje Salming

37 B. **Ted Lindsay**

Few individuals have meant more to hockey than Ted Lindsay. He was never a household name like Gordie Howe or Maurice Richard, but his career, like those of both stars, was measured in equal parts principle and play. If Howe was the goodwill ambassador and Richard the martyred working-class hero, then Lindsay stood for justice. Not only did he mete out his rock-hard brand of hockey on the ice, he never backed down from team managers or even league executives. Today's NHL Players' Association came about through the early efforts of Lindsay, who put his livelihood on the line to form a players' union in the 1950s. When he learned that his Hall of Fame banquet was a males-only affair, he wrote a letter of protest, explaining that his wife had sacrificed a lot to advance his career and that he wanted her there to share in the honor. "If my family can't share in this, I won't go," he said. The Hall refused to budge, and Lindsay boycotted the 1966 ceremony—but he had made his point. The following year, the Hall changed its regulations and admitted women to the gala evening.

Hobey Baker

Fred Maxwell

Frank Rankin

Fred Whitcroft

38 A. The rover

When Brad Richards described Ottawa's Erik Karlsson as "a rover" during the 2012 playoffs, the Rangers captain was referring to Karlsson's inspirational two-way play, the kind of risk-reward hockey made famous by old-time rovers Hobey Baker, Fred "Steamer" Maxwell, Frank Rankin and Fred Whitcroft. They were their team's key icemen, similar to Karlsson's role with the Senators. In seven-man hockey, the rover lined up between the three forwards and two defensemen and became either an extra attacker or an extra defender, picking up a drop pass or rebound on offense and returning to back-check or bodycheck an opposing puck-carrier. While rovers such as Frank McGee, Lester Patrick and Cyclone Taylor all played other offensive or defensive roles after the position was abolished by the NHA in 1910, Baker and his peers became Hall of Famers for roaming the ice primarily as a seventh man.

39 D. 10 or more lines

The best scoring units make a difference every game, but these lines could hurt their opponents every shift. Detroit's Production Line and the Islanders' Long Island Lighting Company became game-changers and dynasty-builders, three-man combos that carried contenders to championships. Among these trios is Montreal's Punch Line, which, despite its fame, played together fewer than five seasons. However, in that short time Toe Blake, Elmer Lach and Maurice Richard revitalized the Canadiens franchise with Stanley Cups in 1944 and 1946 and produced one of hockey's most revered records: Richard's 50-goal season, which was an NHL first. By our count, 11 lines have managed the Hall of Fame hat trick.

The Punch Line: (L—R) Maurice Richard, Elmer Lach and Toe Blake

The Punch Line's Historic 1944—45 Season

NHL Leading Scorers				
Player	Team	GP	Scoring	Honors
Elmer Lach (C)	Montreal	50	26-54-80	Hart, Scoring Leader, 1st All-Star
Maurice Richard (RW)	Montreal	50	50-23-73	1st All-Star
Toe Blake (LW)	Montreal	49	29-38-67	1st All-Star
Bill Cowley	Boston	49	25-40-65	2nd All-Star
Ted Kennedy	Toronto	49	29-25-54	Stanley Cup

40 C. Adam Oates

Based on scoring alone, the most egregious snub for
several years was Adam Oates, who waited five years past
his year of eligibility for his Hall invitation. The greatest
setup center of his generation, Oates earned his unselfish
reputation on two consecutive 100-point seasons, first as
Brett Hull's playmaker in St. Louis and later in partnership
with Cam Neely in Boston, where he amassed a career-
high 142 points in 1992–93. Who knows why all 21 teams
bypassed Oates in the 1985 NHL Entry Draft? In college
hockey he had good numbers and guided Rensselaer
Polytechnic Institute (RPI) to the NCAA title in 1984–85.
While Oates did not become a sensation like Mark
Messier, he was still very good, scoring an imposing 1,420
points between 1985 and 2004, the highest total among
undrafted players. At his 2012 induction, Oates thanked
numerous people and poked fun at himself. Addressing
his wife, Donna, he said, "I love you very much. We met
near the end of my career; I wish we could have met a
little sooner. You could have seen me when I was a little
bit better."

41 How many players returned to NHL action after becoming Hall of Fame members?

A. Only one player, Mario Lemieux

B. Two players

C. Three players

D. Six players

42 Who provided the entertainment for Wayne Gretzky's induction ceremony at the Hall of Fame in 1999?

A.
Shania Twain

B.
Rush

C.
Stompin' Tom Connors

D.
Barenaked Ladies

43 What incident caused Toronto's Conn Smythe to resign as chairman of the Hall of Fame's board in 1971?

A. The Hall's induction of one of Smythe's players

B. A newspaper report investigating Smythe's business dealings

C. Smythe's unpopular trade of a star forward

D. Televised comments Smythe made on *Hockey Night in Canada*

44 Superstars Evgeni Malkin and Ilya Kovalchuk wear sweater numbers honoring which Hall of Fame member?

A.
Brett Hull

B.
Valeri Kharlamov

C.
Jari Kurri

D.
Viacheslav Fetisov

41 C. Three players

Some players retire early and regret it. Others attempt comebacks or stick around too long and tarnish an otherwise distinguished career. Many more leave the game on top. And then there is Gordie Howe, Guy Lafleur and Mario Lemieux. Each quit the game on his own terms and was enshrined in the Hall, only to play again at the NHL level as Hall members. Howe returned a year after his 1972 induction, joining his sons Mark and Marty in the NHL-rival WHA. Lafleur signed with the New York Rangers in September 1988, just weeks after his induction dinner. Lemieux, who first retired in 1997, followed Howe and Lafleur into the history books in December 2000. All three stars still had the legs to compete post-retirement, but as offensive forces, their glory days were over. Lafleur potted an additional 107 points in 165 games during his three seasons; Lemieux scored 229 points in 170 games spread over five frustrating years; and Howe became Methuselah on skates, playing until he was 52 years old. He played six WHA seasons and a complete 80-game NHL season to cap his remarkable career. Although WHA play was a notch below NHL-caliber hockey, Howe netted a combined 549 points in 499 games as a Hall of Famer—a higher total than most pros get in an entire career.

The Comeback Kids of the Hall of Fame

| Player | Induction Year | 1st Career | | | 2nd Career | | | Total NHL GP |
		Years	GP	Scoring	Years	GP	Scoring	
Gordie Howe	1972	1946–1971	1687	786-1023-1809	1979–1980	80	15-26-41	1767
					1973–1979*	419*	174-334-508*	
Guy Lafleur	1988	1971–1985	961	518-728-1246	1988–1991	165	42-65-107	1126
Mario Lemieux	1997	1984–1997	745	613-881-1494	2000–2006	170	77-152-229	915

*Gordie Howe's WHA career

42 C. Stompin' Tom Connors

Seven months after his final NHL game, at Madison Square Garden in April 1999, Wayne Gretzky was feted at a star-studded celebration attended by more than 3,000 friends and fans at the Hall of Fame in Toronto's BCE Place. Before Gretzky took to the stage wearing his new Hall blazer and diamond induction ring, Canadian country music legend Stompin' Tom Connors proudly belted out hockey's unofficial anthem and his signature song, "The Good Old Hockey Game," to hail the Great One's highest honor.

The Kid Line: (L–R) Charlie Conacher, Joe Primeau and Busher Jackson

43 A. The Hall's induction of one of Smythe's players

Conn Smythe assembled one of hockey's most renowned scoring legacies: the Kid Line, made up of Joe Primeau, Charlie Conacher and Busher Jackson. As the center-piece of his rebuilding efforts in Toronto during the late 1920s, the threesome finished first, second and fourth in the 1931–32 scoring race and helped Toronto win its first Stanley Cup under the Maple Leafs banner. While Conacher and Primeau became Hall of Famers in the 1960s, Jackson's entry was blocked by the influential Smythe, who disapproved of his former scoring leader's carousing lifestyle. In 1971, the Hall finally enshrined Jackson, with Smythe resigning from the Hall's selection committee in protest.

44 B. Valeri Kharlamov

Ilya Kovalchuk and Evgeni Malkin weren't yet born when 33-year-old Valeri Kharlamov died in 1981, but, while growing up in Russia, both men were steeped in his fame. Kharlamov was a national hero—a hockey icon of magnificent style and originality. To NHL fans, his slick puck play made him the USSR's most dangerous weapon. The Soviets played a precise puck-control game that rarely allowed for individual creativity, except for the virtuosity of Kharlamov. His threat was so great during the 1972 Summit Series that he received the ultimate compliment: a fractured ankle, courtesy of a vicious premeditated two-hander by Bobby Clarke. NHL teams clamored for his services, yet he was never drafted and never played in the NHL, a result of strict Soviet controls on player movement to North America. Kharlamov's No. 17 defined greatness for Malkin and Kovalchuk, much as NHL fans know No. 9 and No. 99. Kovalchuk wore No. 17 his entire NHL career and reversed the digits, donning No. 71, during international tournaments. Malkin wears No. 71 with the Pittsburgh Penguins and doubles up the ones, sporting No. 11, at the Olympics. Kharlamov was inducted into the Hall in 2005.

The Legendary Valeri Kharlamov

Career Scoring and Medal Stats (1968–1981)			
Competitions	**GP**	**Scoring**	**Team Results**
Olympics	18	15-21-36	Gold (2), Silver (1)
1972 Summit Series	7	3-4-7	Lost vs. Canada (NHL)
Summit of 1974	8	2-5-7	Won vs. Canada (WHA)
NHL Challenge Cup	1	0-1-1	Won vs. NHL All-Stars
Super Series	9	6-4-10	Won 2 series vs. NHL
CSKA / USSR League	436	293-214-507	Gold (11)
Izvestia Cup	55	40-38-78	Gold (9), Silver (2)
World Championships	105	74-82-156	Gold (8), Silver (2), Bronze (1)

Honors: 1976 WC Best Forward, IIHF All-Stars (4), 1972 USSR League MVP, USSR All-Stars (7)

45 Who remarked, "Once the puck drops, you and I are the only two sane men left in the rink"?

A. A referee advising another official

B. A goal judge conferring with his fellow judge

C. A game analyst predicting play to his play-by-play announcer

D. A coach empathizing with the opposing team's coach

46 What disability did Hall of Fame referee Bill Chadwick suffer from during his 1,000-plus-game NHL career?

A. He was unable to read or write

B. He was diagnosed with arrhythmia, an irregular heartbeat

C. He was legally blind in one eye

D. He had a prosthetic limb below his right knee

Team Canada, 1991 World Junior champions

47 Why did Doug Harvey refuse to attend his Hall ceremony in 1973?

A. A fellow inductee that year was once his chief on-ice rival

B. NHL owners had once ostracized him for his union activities

C. He was bitter about the way his NHL career had ended

D. He had wanted immediate entry into the Hall with two other inductees

48 How many different team championships, from junior titles to the NHL and international crowns, has Scott Niedermayer won?

A. Four different championships

B. Five different championships

C. Six different championships

D. Seven different championships

45 A. A referee advising another official

The smallest contingent of Hall inductees resides in the Referees/Linesmen category—a group of fewer than 20 dedicated sportsmen who developed a love of hockey and, despite lacking the skill set to turn pro, never abandoned their passion, becoming the best big-game adjudicators in history. Their dedication is typified by the quality whistle-work of officials such as Andy Van Hellemond, the NHL's number-one mediator for many years and a multiple refereeing record-holder; the colorful Red Storey, a football champion turned hockey zebra and, later, an object of public criticism (which caused his retirement); and Cooper Smeaton, who established his reputation for impartiality with his first call during his first NHL game, when the great Newsy Lalonde challenged him after Smeaton whistled an offside. The novice official fined the superstar five dollars and made his reputation. Hall of Fame referee Mickey Ion may have best described their labors to protégé King Clancy, succinctly observing, "Once the puck drops, you and I are the only two sane men left in the rink."

Whistle Blowers: (L–R) King Clancy, Mickey Ion and Bill Stewart

46 C. He was legally blind in one eye

Although an errant puck to his right eye cost Bill Chadwick a playing career, he never lost sight of making the NHL—or of making a joke about being a visually impaired referee. As he told it, "I used to get a chuckle in a game when I'd hear a fan yell, 'You're blind, Chadwick.' I knew they were half right." Still, with 20/20 vision in his left eye, Chadwick called more than 1,000 games and pioneered the first system of hand signals for penalties. For a holding call, he grabbed his wrist, for slashing he chopped at his forearm and for tripping he made a karate-like motion against his knee. It was a spontaneous gesture because "there was so much noise that I had difficulty communicating with the penalty timekeeper," Chadwick once told the Associated Press. Ironically, a half-blind referee established a visual means of communicating penalty calls that has become the standard throughout the hockey world. Chadwick was the first American-born official inducted into the Hall. His call came in 1964.

Bill Chadwick

Doug Harvey

47 D. He had wanted immediate entry into the Hall with two other inductees

Doug Harvey played by his own rules, on and off the ice—a rebel with many causes. Harvey was a principal visionary of the first players' union, but when he boycotted his 1973 Hall celebration, he did it because he believed his induction should have coincided with Gordie Howe and Jean Béliveau's in 1972. Howe and Béliveau sidestepped the usual three-year wait after retirement, and Harvey, considered the best defenseman of all time next to Bobby Orr, felt entitled to that same recognition after playing his last game in 1969. It was just Harvey's dark side. After his first Stanley Cup, in 1953, he refused to shake hands with the Boston Bruins, stating without regret, "I'm running them into the boards and banging them around one minute and because we win the Stanley Cup, that's going to change? I don't really like them anyway. Why should I shake their hands?"

48 C. Six different championships

It is neither by accident nor by luck that Scott Niedermayer is the game's all-time greatest champion. As coach Ken Hitchcock noted, his kind of success came from making the players around him better, and his competitiveness was extraordinary, especially at hockey's greatest showcases. "Whenever the game mattered the most, he was always the best player on the ice on either team," said Hitchcock. "Winning follows winning. From the day he showed up as a 16-year-old in Kamloops until the day he retired in the NHL, all he did was win." Niedermayer wasted little time in claiming Hall membership. He was inducted on his first try in 2013.

Scott Niedermayer: Hockey's Biggest Winner

Title	Wins
World Junior Championship	1 (Canada, 1991)
Memorial Cup	1 (Kamloops, 1992)
Stanley Cup	4 (New Jersey, 1995, 2000, 2003; Anaheim, 2007)
Olympic Gold	2 (Canada, 2002, 2010)
IIHF World Championship	1 (Canada, 2004)
World Cup of Hockey	1 (Canada, 2004)

Honors: Memorial Cup MVP (1992), NHL All-Rookie Team (1993), James Norris (2004), Stanley Cup MVP (2007), NHL 1st All-Star (2004, 2006, 2007)

Scott Niedermayer

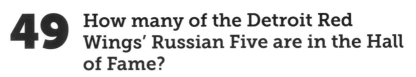

Questions 49-52

49

How many of the Detroit Red Wings' Russian Five are in the Hall of Fame?

A.
Two players

B.
Three players

C.
Four players

D.
All five players

50

Who is the only rearguard to win the Hart Trophy since Bobby Orr in 1972?

A.
Chris Pronger of the
St. Louis Blues

B.
Nicklas Lidstrom of the
Detroit Red Wings

C.
Zdeno Chara of the
Boston Bruins

D.
Phil Housley of the
Winnipeg Jets

51 Despite scoring in more games than any other player during the eight-game 1972 Summit Series, this individual is not in the Hall of Fame. Who is he?

A.
Alexander
Yakushev of
the USSR

B.
Dennis Hull
of Canada

C.
Paul Henderson
of Canada

D.
Vladimir Petrov
of the USSR

52 Class of 2015 Hall inductee Nicklas Lidstrom accomplished which of these NHL firsts?

A. The first defenseman since Bobby Orr to win three consecutive James Norris Trophies

B. The first European-trained NHLer to captain a Stanley Cup champion team

C. The first European-trained NHLer to win the Conn Smythe Trophy as playoff MVP

D. All of the above

49 B. Three players

Igor Larionov

If the Hall of Fame ever broadens its induction guidelines to create a special category for scoring units, it could start with Detroit's feared Russian Five of Igor Larionov, Vladimir Konstantinov, Viacheslav Fetisov, Vyacheslav Kozlov and Sergei Fedorov. Assembled by coach Scotty Bowman, from a suggestion by Larionov, the quintet of skaters imitated old Soviet-era teams, which frequently combined forwards and defensemen as five-man units. Backed by its combination of speed, imagination and puck control, the Red Wings blitzed the league with a record 62 wins in 1995–96 and rolled to back-to-back championships in 1997 and 1998. "My main trick was not to unite all five Russians every time," Bowman told nhl.com. "Often I would wait until the second or even third period to get them out on the ice together. It always got other teams confused." Shortly after the 1997 Cup, Konstantinov suffered life-threatening and career-ending injuries in a car accident, ending the Russian Five's success but inspiring the Wings to another Cup. To date, Larionov, Fetisov and Fedorov have been enshrined with Hall of Fame membership.

Viacheslav Fetisov

Sergei Fedorov

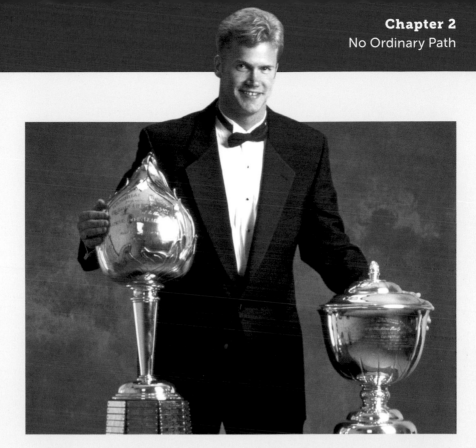

50 A. Chris Pronger of the St. Louis Blues

Blending physical play with offensive intuition and scary skill is what made Chris Pronger a world-class athlete in the NHL. His defensive reads were uncanny and he patrolled the point like a shark circling its prey. On the attack he had the menace of a street thug. At no time was his dominance more evident than in 1999–2000, when the 6-foot-6 St. Louis rearguard led the league in plus-minus (plus-52), topped his Blues in assists (48), finished second among all defensemen and third on his team in points (62), came in third on his team in penalty minutes (92) and averaged a huge 30:14 of ice time through 79 games. St. Louis finished first overall with an all-time club high of 114 points, and the team posted the league's third-highest goal count (248) while allowing the fewest goals (165). Hart Trophy voters defied the tradition of bestowing the MVP title on a big-goal forward and instead handed it to Pronger, the first defender so honored since Bobby Orr in 1972.

51 C. Paul Henderson of Canada

The most-debated Hall candidate in recent memory is Paul Henderson. The 13-year NHL veteran had a solid but unspectacular career, garnering no individual trophies, All-Star selections or championships. However, at the epic Summit Series against the Soviet Union in 1972, Henderson became the most reliable goal scorer among the world's top players, riding a hot streak with goals in six of the tournament's eight games. No one, including series star Phil Esposito and Soviet great Alexander Yakushev, scored in more matches.

The 29-year-old winger tallied once in Game 1's disastrous loss, had the equalizer in Game 3's 4–4 tie, netted two goals in the pivotal Game 5 (which Canada still lost, but proved to be the series turning point) and then posted consecutive game winners in Games 6, 7 and 8. The series winner came off Henderson's stick with just 34 seconds remaining in the final game. So the debate goes on. If Summit Series–losing goalie Vladislav Tretiak is in the Hall, why isn't the player who beat him seven times in eight games a Hall of Famer too?

The Case for Paul Henderson

Professional Record (1962–1980)									
Regular Season					Playoffs				
League	GP	Scoring	+/−	PIM	GP	Scoring	+/−	PIM
NHL	707	236-241-477	+89	304	56	11-14-25		28
WHA	360	140-143-283	−9	112	5	1-1-2	−4	0
Total	1067	376-384-760	+80	416	61	12-15-27		28

1972 Summit Series Record									
GP	Scoring	+/−	SOG	Shot %	PIM	ESG	PPG	SHG	GWG
8	7-3-10*	6	27	25.9	4	7	0	0	3

*Official record—Recent game reviews suggest that Henderson's record of 7-3-10 should include one more point, an assist on Canada's first goal in Game 8.

Nicklas Lidstrom

52 D. All of the above

When the hockey world said thank you to Nicklas Lidstrom for 20 years of game-breaking NHL hockey upon his retirement in 2012, teammates remembered him as "The Perfect Human." Lidstrom combined elite ability with ironman durability. His puck-carrying and shooting skills were masterful, eclipsed only by his brand of defense, which would strip an opponent of the puck to create a turnover rather than deliver the big body blow. Lidstrom's penalty totals were so low that in 2000–01 he tied old-time rearguard Red Kelly for the lowest box time by a Norris Trophy winner, with just 18 minutes. Lidstrom also finished runner-up on five occasions in Lady Byng voting as the league's cleanest player—no easy task while playing a position seldom distinguished for its gentlemanly conduct. Lidstrom filled the back of his hockey card with four Stanley Cup titles, seven Norris awards, one Conn Smythe Trophy as playoff MVP and 11 NHL All-Star Game appearances. He was an inspirational leader and Detroit's captain for six seasons.

Action Heroes

• •

Working the left wing for 16 years, Hall inductee Bob Gainey was your typical defensive forward— nothing flashy, almost inconspicuous. However, Gainey excelled in every aspect of the game to become hockey's best all-round two-way player, scoring key goals, shutting down scoring threats and providing gritty leadership. After the NHL created the Frank Selke Trophy for the position, Gainey won the first four trophies, a total no other player has matched. In this game, match the players with their sometimes-forgotten achievements.

For solutions, turn the page.

Steve Yzerman · Adam Oates · Pierre Pilote · Larry Robinson · Ray Bourque · Tim Horton · Bobby Hull

Part 1

1. [   ] The NHL's all-time leader in career plus-minus.

2. [   ] He was named a new NHL head coach and a Hall of Famer on the same day.

3. [   ] He is the NHL sniper most closely identified with the first rules limiting the maximum allowable curve of a stick blade.

4. [   ] He was the founder of a small doughnut and coffee shop in Hamilton, Ontario, that has become a giant Canadian franchise operation branded with "Always Fresh."

5. [   ] He fired the highest shot count on goal both in one NHL game and in an NHL career.

6. [_____] He is the only player to wait 17 years before receiving his First All-Star Team selection.

7. [_____] Before Bobby Orr, Larry Robinson and Scott Niedermayer, he was the first NHL defenseman to lead the playoffs in scoring.

Patrick Roy   Eddie Shore   Gordie Howe   Tiny Thompson

Reg Noble   Michel Goulet   Bernie Geoffrion

Part 2

1. [_____] He scored the most career goals in NHL action without netting a 50-goal season.

2. [_____] Asked by reporters why he stared at his net after the national anthem, this rookie netminder responded in broken English "I was talking to my goalposts."

3. [_____] An agreement between an NHL team and his own AHL franchise allowed him to play defense in two pro leagues simultaneously in 1939–40.

4. [_____] He was the last active player from the NHL's first season of 1917–18.

5. [_____] Among 50-goal scorers, he recorded the most game winners in one season while also having the lowest goal total.

6. [_____] In one NHL playoff match he set a league record with 113 saves, through regulation time and six overtime periods.

7. [_____] He established what is almost certainly an unbeatable NHL record of 53 consecutive games in the Stanley Cup Final.

Action Heroes
Solutions

Part 1

1. Defenseman **Larry Robinson** built his NHL-best plus-730 over 20 years. He never had a minus season, recording a plus-120 in 1976–77. Nine of the league's top 10 plus-minus men are Hall of Famers.

2. June 26, 2012, was a career day for **Adam Oates**. Just 15 minutes after Washington hired him as its 16th head coach, Oates received a second phone call, this one from the Hall.

3. He wasn't the first shooter with a curved stick, but **Bobby Hull** owned the most celebrated "banana blade." In 1967–68, the NHL reduced the maximum allowable curve to 1 inch and then again to ½ inch in 1970–1971.

4. **Tim Horton** went far beyond the one-dimensional defensive game he was taught. In business, it was no different, defying doubters to start a retail chain called Tim Hortons before dying tragically in February 1974.

5. In 22 seasons, **Ray Bourque** rarely averaged fewer than 200 shots per year to amass an NHL career-high of 6,206. His best game was a league-record 19-shot effort in March 1991. It's believed that Gordie Howe shares Bourque's lead with his own 19-shot night in January 1955.

6. **Steve Yzerman** had six consecutive 100-point seasons, yet his First All-Star Team berth didn't come until he was 35, when he notched 79 points in 1999–2000, his 17th NHL season.

7. Only a few rearguards have become postseason scoring leaders. In 1961, **Pierre Pilote** topped all Chicago gunners, including Bobby Hull and Stan Mikita, to tie Gordie Howe as playoff leader, by scoring 15 points.

Part 2

1. **Gordie Howe** amassed his monster 801-goal count without ever reaching the 50-goal plateau in NHL play. His closest total came when he scored 49 in 1952–53.

2. Dubbed St. Patrick by the media for his miraculous goaltending, **Patrick Roy** later explained when his English improved that he really doesn't speak to his posts, he simply envisioned his net getting smaller.

3. In his final NHL year, **Eddie Shore** played home games for the New York Americans and his own club, the AHL Springfield Indians. On many nights, the 37-year-old Shore had back-to-back games, commuting between cities to meet his obligations.

4. No player from the NHL's debut season of 1917–18 played longer than **Reg Noble**, the last of the original NHLers. He broke into the NHL with the Toronto Arenas in 1917–18 and played for 16 seasons, until 1932–33.

5. **Michel Goulet**'s best season came in 1983–84, when he scored 56 goals and 121 points. He notched 16 game winners for a Quebec Nordiques club that won 42 games. He owns the highest percentage of game winners among 50-goal men, 28.6 percent.

6. On April 3, 1933, Boston's **Tiny Thompson** broke the triple-digit barrier with 113 saves in a 1–0 Toronto win. Maple Leafs goalie Lorne Chabot turned back 93 shots. They combined to stop 206 shots, playing 164 minutes and 46 seconds.

7. Between 1951 and 1960 there were a total of 53 games in the Stanley Cup Final, and Montreal's **Bernie Geoffrion** was the only player to appear in every match during that 10-year stretch. He had 46 points in 53 straight games.

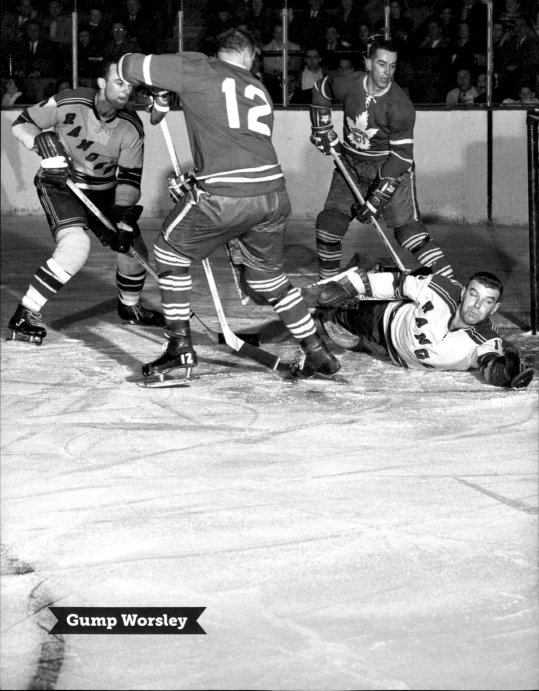

Gump Worsley

Class Acts

Firsts and Onlys

Since its inception, the Hall of Fame has always been more than just about one league. While most Hall members come from the NHL, their backgrounds and journeys to greatness are truly unique. Take Gump Worsley. Few Hall of Famers yo-yoed between the NHL and the minor leagues as much as the Gumper. Despite his circuitous route to immortality, he was a star in every home rink he played and the first and only goalie to be named a First-Team All-Star in six different major leagues: the Quebec Junior Hockey League (1949), the Eastern Hockey League (1950), the United States Hockey League (1951), the Western Hockey League (1954), the American Hockey League (1964) and the NHL (1968).

53 Which scoring line first had all its members elected to the Hall of Fame?

A. The Kid Line of the Toronto Maple Leafs

B. The Production Line of the Detroit Red Wings

C. The Flying Frenchmen Line of the Montreal Canadiens

D. The Long Island Lighting Company of the New York Islanders

54 Who was the first European-trained NHLer in Hall history?

A.
Peter Stastny of Czechoslovakia

B.
Viacheslav Fetisov of the USSR

C.
Borje Salming of Sweden

D.
Jari Kurri of Finland

55 Who were the first inductees from the goaltending fraternity to enter the Hall of Fame in 1945?

A.
Charlie Gardiner
and Georges Vezina

B.
Georges Vezina
and Alex Connell

C.
Alex Connell
and George Hainsworth

D.
George Hainsworth
and Charlie Gardiner

56 When were the first female players honored in the Hall of Fame?

- **A.** 1998
- **B.** 2002
- **C.** 2006
- **D.** 2010

53 C. The Flying Frenchmen Line of the Montreal Canadiens

Montreal rearguards Didier Pitre and Jack Laviolette possessed such speed and strength that they were dubbed the Flying Frenchmen, a nickname that later became synonymous with the Canadiens when the defensive duo was paired on a forward line with the supersonic Newsy Lalonde. Their end-to-end rushes and skill at putting the puck in the net led Montreal to its first Stanley Cup, in 1916. The trio's moniker soon came to define the Canadiens' high-scoring brand of hockey—an irony, considering that style of freewheeling offense was inspired by one-time blue-liners. With the inductions of Pitre and Laviolette in 1962—Lalonde had been honored in 1950—the first scoring line made its grand entrance into the Hall.

Scoring Lines in the Hall of Fame

Line	Team	Linemates (Induction Years)		
Flying Frenchmen	Montreal	Newsy Lalonde (1950)	Jack Laviolette (1962)	Didier Pitre (1962)
Pony Line	Chicago	Doug Bentley (1964)	Max Bentley (1966)	Bill Mosienko (1965)
Punch Line	Montreal	Toe Blake (1966)	Elmer Lach (1966)	Maurice Richard (1961)
Kid Line	Toronto	Charlie Conacher (1961)	Busher Jackson (1971)	Joe Primeau (1963)
S Line	Mtl. Maroons	Babe Siebert (1964)	Hooley Smith (1972)	Nels Stewart (1952)
Production Line	Detroit	Sid Abel (1969)	Gordie Howe (1972)	Ted Lindsay (1966)
A Line	NY Rangers	Frank Boucher (1958)	Bill Cook (1952)	Bun Cook (1995)
Production Line 2	Detroit	Alex Delvecchio (1977)	Gordie Howe (1972)	Frank Mahovlich (1981)
Dynasty Line	Montreal	Guy Lafleur (1988)	Jacques Lemaire (1984)	Steve Shutt (1993)
Kraut Line	Boston	Bobby Bauer (1996)	Woody Dumart (1992)	Milt Schmidt (1961)
Long Island Lighting Co.	NY Islanders	Mike Bossy (1991)	Clark Gillies (2002)	Bryan Trottier (1997)

54 C. Borje Salming of Sweden

Borje Salming changed hockey the way Jackie Robinson impacted baseball, and here's why. Salming, like Robinson in his sport, became a trailblazer in an unprecedented movement that revolutionized the demographic makeup of North American hockey. Today, long after Salming's arrival in 1973–74, almost 20 percent of the league is born and trained in Europe. During his 17-year NHL tenure, Salming turned Euro-bashers into believers, persevering through verbal baiting and bullying tactics to play 1,148 games and become a superstar defenseman. His determination, grace and skill under fire made an everlasting impression on North American audiences. Although Salming never won a Stanley Cup, it's hard to imagine a European not playing on a championship team today. Fittingly, the European who opened up the NHL pioneered the way into the Hall of Fame. Salming broke through in 1996.

Borje Salming—European Trailblazer

NHL Career Stats (1973–1990)									
Regular Season									
GP	Scoring Stats	PIM	Shots	S%	Plus-Minus*				
					TGF	PGF	TGA	PGA	+/-
1148	150-637-787	1344	2536	5.9	2111	580	1977	621	175

NHL Playoff Stats (1973–1988)			International (select)				
			Olympics		Canada Cup		
GP	Scoring Stats	PIM	GP	Scoring Stats	GP	Scoring Stats	
81	12-37-49	91	8	4-3-7	16	4-5-9	

*hockey-reference.com numbers. Subtract total goals for (TGF) from power-play goals for (PGF). Subtract total goals against (TGA) from power-play goals against (PGA). Subtract those two totals for the career plus-minus.

55 A. Charlie Gardiner and Georges Vezina

Among such legends as Howie Morenz, Hobey Baker and Lord Stanley, two goalies made the grade when the Hockey Hall of Fame began in 1945. Georges Vezina and Charlie Gardiner left indelible marks on hockey history and exited the game under tragic circumstances, their careers and lives cut short, Vezina from tuberculosis in 1925 and Gardiner, himself a two-time Vezina Trophy winner with Chicago, of a brain hemorrhage shortly after backstopping the Black Hawks to their first Stanley Cup in 1934. After Vezina and Gardiner were inducted in 1945, no other starting goalie entered the Hall until 1958.

Georges Vezina and Charlie Gardiner (right)

Angela James

Cammi Granato

56 D. 2010

The Hall of Fame made gender equality a priority in 2010, when it amended its bylaws to welcome women into the 65-year-old institution. The Hall's 18-member, all-male committee honored four-time world champion Angela James of Canada and 1998 U.S. gold medalist Cammi Granato. James and Granato, once fierce on-ice rivals, will be linked forever for their historic breakthrough, James the first female superstar of modern hockey and Granato the most-recognized American woman in the game in the 1990s. "I am in awe that I'm standing here!" Granato said. "You're changing the face of women's hockey by accepting us into this prestigious club." James and Granato graduated with fellow 2010 classmate Dino Ciccarelli, the Hall's 245th male player.

57 Which Hall of Fame goalie never recorded a winning regular season in NHL play?

A.
Hap Holmes

B.
Chuck Rayner

C.
Glenn Hall

D.
Eddie Giacomin

58 Though Wayne Gretzky popularized it, he wasn't the first to make plays behind opponents' nets. Which Hall of Famer is credited with first employing this tactic?

A.
Bernie Federko

B.
Bryan Trottier

C.
Jacques Lemaire

D.
Bobby Clarke

59 Who was the first NHL draft pick to be nominated to the Hall of Fame?

A.
Brad Park

B.
Gilbert Perreault

C.
Ken Dryden

D.
Darryl Sittler

60 The only Hall of Famer drafted twice into the NHL came from which country?

A.
United States

B.
USSR

C.
Czech Republic

D.
Canada

57 B. Chuck Rayner

Few top-end puckstoppers experienced greater team ineptitude than Chuck Rayner. Simply, Rayner gave much more than he got back from the teams he defended. His fans knew it, so too did the Hall of Fame selection committee at his induction in 1973. His curse was a career in New York, first with the lowly Americans and then the struggling Rangers, where the closest he came to icing a winning season was his 28-30-11 record of 1949–50. Despite those grim totals, Rayner was named league MVP and carried his plucky Blueshirts to within one goal of the Stanley Cup. After battling hard through two overtime matches to keep ahead of Detroit in the final round, he surrendered the heartbreaker in double overtime in Game 7, the Cup goal from Wings winger Pete Babando. History will remember it as the NHL's first overtime tally in a seventh game of the final. Although he posted more victories than losses that postseason, Rayner remains the only Hall of Fame goalie without a winning regular season.

Chuck Rayner: New York's Silver Lining

Goalie Stats (1949–50)							
Regular Season				Playoffs			
GP	Record	GAA	SO	GP	Record	GAA	SO
69	28-30-11	2.62	6	12	7-5	2.25	1

Career Goalie Stats (1940–1953)							
Regular Season				Playoffs			
GP	Record	GAA	SO	GP	Record	GAA	SO
424	138-208-77	3.05	25	18	9-9	2.43	1

58 D. Bobby Clarke

The heart and soul of the 1970s Philadelphia Flyers was Bobby Clarke, captain of that band of hell-raisers and bangers known as the Broad Street Bullies. They perfected strategic intimidation and went on to become the first post-1967 expansion team to win the Stanley Cup, in 1974 and again in 1975. But the brawling Flyers also won with superb goaltending from Bernie Parent, the offensive punch of 50-goal scorer Rick MacLeish and the gritty pivot Clarke, who was the team's workhorse and spark plug as well as a three-time Hart Trophy MVP during the team's heyday. Among Clarke's craftiest moves was his play behind an opponent's net. That caught the eye of Wayne Gretzky's Junior B coach Gene Popeil, who suggested that his 14-year old prodigy do the same to fend off the 19-year-olds who were slamming him around at the crease. Gretzky soon made it his "office" in the NHL, but Clarke (and others such as Bernie Federko) occupied it first.

59 C. Ken Dryden

Few events shaped the storied rivalry between Boston and Montreal like the 1971 Stanley Cup playoffs. During an NHL-record run of 18 consecutive playoff series losses to the Canadiens—between 1943 and 1987—the Bruins looked set to snap the Habs' spell in the 1971 quarterfinals. Boston was the defending Cup champion and had the dynastic core of Bobby Orr and Phil Esposito. The team's bench of marksmen claimed the first, second, third and fourth spots in regular-season scoring in a year when seven of the league's best 11 scorers were Bruins. Meanwhile, Montreal had finished 24 points back of first-place Boston and decided to stake its postseason fortunes on a college goalie named Ken Dryden. Without much exaggeration, the B's were already planning a parade route and their roster list for the Cup engravers. But the underdog Canadiens won it all with Dryden, a 1964 draft pick, originally selected by—wait for it—Boston.

First Drafted Players to Enter the Hall of Fame*

Player	Induction Year	Team	Overall Draft Pick	Draft Year	Career Scoring
Ken Dryden	1983	Boston	14th	1964	258-57-74**
Bobby Clarke	1987	Philadelphia	17th	1969	358-852-1210
Guy Lafleur	1988	Montreal	1st	1971	560-793-1353
Brad Park	1988	NY Rangers	2nd	1966	213-683-896
Darryl Sittler	1989	Toronto	8th	1970	484-637-1121
Vladislav Tretiak	1989	Montreal	143rd	1983	dnp

dnp = Did not play in NHL

*All selections since the NHL's first amateur draft in 1963

**Goalie W-L-T stats

Viacheslav Fetisov

60 B. USSR

Even before his distinguished NHL career, Viacheslav Fetisov was destined for the Hall of Fame. His international triumphs as an elite Soviet defender were unmatched. He claimed multiple gold medals at the World Juniors then at the World Championships, where he pocketed six golds and was named a tournament All-Star nine times. At the Olympics he earned two more golds and a silver, and he appeared in two Canada Cups, including the Soviets' surprise victory in 1981. Trying to land Fetisov, NHL teams twice chanced draft picks on the defenseman Wayne Gretzky said was "the best I ever played against." Fetisov was selected 201st overall by Montreal in 1978 and then 150th by New Jersey five years later, in the 1983 draft. Few expected Fetisov to ever play for the Devils, but when freedom finally came in 1989, he made his NHL appearance at 31. His exceptional coordination and mobility kept him playing in the world's best league for nine more years, a winner with two Stanley Cups rings from Detroit, in 1997 and 1998.

61 Boston great Dit Clapper is credited with what Hall of Fame first at his 1947 induction?

A.
He was the first living honoree

B.
He was the first non-North American inductee

C.
He was the first to wait 20 years for Hall membership

D.
He was the first NHLer enshrined in the Hall

62 Who was the only goalie welcomed into the Hall without the customary three-year waiting period?

A.
Jacques Plante

B.
Terry Sawchuk

C.
Bernie Parent

D.
Grant Fuhr

63 The first Russian-born Hall inductee was honored in which year?

A.
1962

B.
1975

C.
1985

D.
1989

64 Which Hall of Famer was the first to have his own Hall of Fame?

A.
Maurice Richard

B.
Bobby Orr

C.
Wayne Gretzky

D.
Mario Lemieux

61. A. He was the first living honoree

Dit Clapper's title as the first active Hall of Famer came by circumstance, since all the original inductees in 1945, pioneers such as Frank McGee, Eddie Gerard and Hod Stuart, were elected posthumously. The next induction, in 1947, added seven living players, Clapper among them. Six honorees, including the mythic Eddie Shore and Aurèle Joliat, were officially welcomed into the Hall on February 25, two weeks after Clapper was honored in a special ceremony at his final NHL match, on February 12.

Dit Clapper

62 B. Terry Sawchuk

Based on the individuals who broke his records, Terry Sawchuk was one extraordinary goalie. He surrendered the NHL's two greatest netminding records to the game's greatest set of puckstoppers: Patrick Roy and Martin Brodeur. But it didn't happen overnight. It took three decades before Roy smashed Sawchuk's career mark of 447 wins, in 2000–01. Almost a decade after that, Brodeur finally eclipsed 103 shutouts, a Sawchuk record most experts considered unassailable. Sawchuk stopped playing in 1969–70 and was enshrined, posthumously, in 1971, months after his death from heart failure following surgery that was the result of a backyard fight with teammate Ron Stewart. Sawchuk is the only goalie to gain immediate admittance into the Hall.

117

63 A. 1962

Little-known Val Hoffinger was the first Russian in the NHL, but it wasn't until Sweeney Schriner made his debut in 1934–35 that the USSR had a bona fide Hall of Fame contender. Schriner, a native of Saratov, Russia, went on to score 405 points in a 484-game career. However, considering his parents moved to Canada when he was one year old, his native country had very little to do with his on-ice success in North America. In his newly adopted land, Schriner learned to skate, shoot and pass, quickly developing into an NHL star and winning the 1935 Calder Trophy as top rookie. He then won successive league scoring titles in 1935–36 and 1936–37. His high-profile trade to Toronto for five players in 1939 brought him his greatest success: two Stanley Cups. He entered the Hall in 1962, more than 25 years before Vladislav Tretiak was welcomed as the first Russian-trained player.

Sweeney Schriner

The Best NHL Years of Sweeney Schriner

Season	Team	GP		Scoring		Honors
		RS	PS	RS	PS	
1934–35	NY Americans	48	0	18-22-40	dnp	Top rookie
1935–36	NY Americans	48	5	19-26-45	3-1-4	Top scorer, 1st All-Star
1936–37	NY Americans	48	0	21-25-46	dnp	Top scorer, 2nd All-Star
1938–39	NY Americans	48	2	13-31-44	0-0-0	Scoring race runner-up
1940–41	Toronto	48	7	24-14-38	2-1-3	1st All-Star
1941–42	Toronto	47	13	20-16-36	6-3-9	Stanley Cup
1944–45	Toronto	26	13	22-15-37	3-1-4	Stanley Cup

64 B. Bobby Orr

In July 2003, the first Hall of Fame dedicated to one hockey player had its grand opening in Parry Sound, Ontario. The museum is devoted to all things achieved by hometown hero Bobby Orr, who appeared at the event and gave an emotional speech expressing his thanks. On exhibit at his Hall of Fame is a wide selection of memorabilia from his playing days. Each year the facility's selection committee accepts nominations for the induction of athletes with a direct connection to the Parry Sound area.

65 When did the Hall of Fame first elect an American-born member?

A. In 1945, at its inaugural induction

B. In 1955, 10 years after its first induction

C. In 1965, 20 years after its first induction

D. In 1975, 30 years after its first induction

66 Who was the first female player to score a goal in a men's professional league?

A.
Nancy Drolet

B.
Cassie Campbell

C.
Hayley Wickenheiser

D.
Danielle Goyette

67 Which Hall of Fame brothers were the only siblings to finish among the top-three scorers during an NHL season?

A.
George and Frank Boucher

B.
Maurice and Henri Richard

C.
Charlie and Roy Conacher

D.
Max and Doug Bentley

68 Which scoring line of Hall of Famers was the first to finish 1, 2, 3 in an NHL scoring race?

A. New York's A Line of Frank Boucher and Bill and Bun Cook

B. Detroit's Production Line of Gordie Howe, Ted Lindsay and Sid Abel

C. Montreal's Punch Line of Maurice Richard, Elmer Lach and Toe Blake

D. Boston's Kraut Line of Milt Schmidt, Woody Dumart and Bobby Bauer

65 A. In 1945, at its inaugural induction

In its first year, the Hall of Fame inducted eight Canadians (with one born in Scotland, Charlie Gardiner) and Pennsylvania native Hobey Baker. Handsome and privileged, Baker was regarded as the best all-around athlete at Princeton and the greatest player in U.S. hockey while skating in the NCAA, from 1911 to 1914. After graduating, he worked on Wall Street and starred in the amateur ranks. Baker never turned pro, playing purely for the love of the game because, as some said, he could afford to. During the First World War, he became an ace pilot and survived combat, only to be killed in an airplane crash just days after the armistice was signed in 1918. Baker is the only man elected to both the College Football Hall of Fame and the Hockey Hall of Fame.

Hobey Baker

66 C. Hayley Wickenheiser

Several elite female players merit Hall recognition. However, few have achieved as much athletically and contributed more to the growth of women's hockey than Hayley Wickenheiser. She has been the face of women's hockey for almost 20 years and Canada's most dangerous and most consistent player through six gold medals at the IIHF Women's World Championships and four golds and one silver at the Olympics, all while distinguishing herself as an Olympic tournament MVP in 2002 and 2006 and a multiple Olympic record-holder in goals, assists and points. She has been called the "female Wayne Gretzky," but she is really a blend of Gretzky and Al MacInnis because of her speed, finesse and lethal slap shot—a blast that many consider the hardest in the women's game. Bobby Clarke was so impressed with her performance at the 1998 Olympics that he invited her twice to Philadelphia's rookie camps. Later, in 2002, Phil Esposito offered her a 15-game tryout with the ECHL's Cincinnati Cyclones. She declined both invites, choosing the more open and less physical game in Europe, with Kirkkonummen Salamat, a Division 2 club in Finland. Her historic goal came in a 5–4 loss on February 1, 2003. "I had something to prove," said Wickenheiser, who played on boys' teams until she was 12 years old.

67 D. Max and Doug Bentley

The Richards are the odds-on favorite in this category, considering both were frequent top-10 snipers during their lengthy NHL stints. But because of a 15-year age difference, Maurice's career as a leading scorer was almost over just as Henri's was taking off, so they never produced a top-10 finish in the same year. The famous Boucher family of Ottawa had four siblings in pro hockey at one time during the 1920s, and although George and Frank are Hall of Famers, it was George and Billy (not a Hall member) who finished second and third in 1923–24's scoring race. However, in 1942–43, Doug and Max Bentley (pictured, Doug is on the left), playing on Chicago's Pony Line together, scored first and third finishes with Doug's league-high 73 points and Max's third-place 70 points. They are the only brother act in the Hall with an NHL top-three finish. Max would later star for the Toronto Maple Leafs, and the brothers would play one more season together in 1953–54, as members of the New York Rangers.

Black Hawk Brothers in Arms:
The Bentleys of 1942–43

NHL Leading Scorers				
Player	Team	GP	Scoring	Honors
Doug Bentley	Chicago	50	33-40-73	Top scorer, 1st All-Star
Bill Cowley	Boston	48	27-45-72	Hart, 1st All-Star
Max Bentley	Chicago	47	26-44-70	Lady Byng
Lynn Patrick	NY Rangers	50	22-39-61	2nd All-Star
Lorne Carr	Toronto	50	27-33- 60	1st All-Star

68 D. Boston's Kraut Line of Milt Schmidt, Woody Dumart and Bobby Bauer

Only three lines sported players who finished 1, 2, 3 in the NHL scoring race—and all came from the Original Six era or earlier. Each member of those units became a Hall of Famer, including those on the Production Line (who topped the scoring race in 1949–50), the Punch Line (tops in 1944–45) and the first top-three trio, the Kraut Line of 1939–40. Boston formed its potent line of Milt Schmidt (No. 15), Woody Dumart (No. 14) and Bobby Bauer (No. 17) in 1937–38. Almost immediately, they became known as the Kraut Line, a reference to their Germanic hometown of Berlin, later called Kitchener, in southern Ontario. The line piloted the Bruins to the 1939 and 1941 Stanley Cups, and in 1939–40 they paced the league in scoring. Schmidt was inducted in 1961, Dumart in 1992 and Bauer in 1996.

The Kraut Line's Podium Finish

1939–40 NHL Leading Scorers				
Player	Team	GP	Scoring	Honors
Milt Schmidt	Boston	48	22-30-52	Top scorer, 1st All-Star
Woody Dumart	Boston	48	22-21-43	2nd All-Star
Bobby Bauer	Boston	48	17-26-43	Lady Byng, 2nd All-Star
Gordie Drillon	Toronto	43	21-19-40	4th in scoring race
Bill Cowley	Boston	48	13-27-40	5th in scoring race

69 A few Soviet-trained individuals were enshrined in the Hall of Fame before Detroit defenseman Viacheslav Fetisov's induction in 2001. Who was first?

A. The goalie who never played NHL hockey, Vladislav Tretiak

B. The dictatorial head coach of the national team, Viktor Tikhonov

C. Fetisov's teammate and Stanley Cup winner Igor Larionov

D. The legendary founder of Russian hockey, Anatoli Tarasov

70 Who is the only NHL goalie inducted as a Builder?

A.
George
Hainsworth

B.
Emile
Francis

C.
Patrick
Roy

D.
Harry
Lumley

71 Inducted together in their first year of eligibility, when did defensive greats Ray Bourque, Paul Coffey and Larry Murphy become Hall members?

A. 2003   **B.** 2004

C. 2005   **D.** 2006

72 Who in the Hall of Fame was the NHL's first European-trained player drafted first overall?

A.
Peter Forsberg of Sweden

B.
Pavel Bure of the USSR

C.
Mats Sundin of Sweden

D.
Dominik Hasek of Czechoslovakia

69 D. The legendary founder of Russian hockey, Anatoli Tarasov

Viacheslav Fetisov was not the first Soviet enshrined in the Hall. His induction in 2001 came 12 years after Vladislav Tretiak's in 1989 and 27 years after Anatoli Tarasov was welcomed as a Builder in 1974. Tarasov's prominence in the sport can't be overstated. As the architect of Soviet hockey, he developed a national team program from scratch and built it into an international powerhouse that ended Canada's amateur dominance and shifted the balance of power in the hockey world.

Anatoli Tarasov

70 B. Emile Francis

Few players are elected to the Builder category. Typically, inductees' bladed exploits determine their Hall status, regardless of what they accomplish later, as hockey executives. Goalie Emile Francis proved to be an exception, platooning 17 years in the minor pros with NHL stops for coffee in Chicago and New York, where he played 95 games from 1946 to 1952. His NHL career goals-against average of 3.76 impressed few, but Francis contributed mightily to the netminding fraternity when he took a first baseman's mitt and sewed on a protective cuff. His hybrid creation became hockey's first trapper in 1947–48. Later, Francis found his true calling when he entered the Rangers' system as a coach and general manager, an association that lasted more than a decade. In New York he also started the Metropolitan Junior League, an enterprise that fostered numerous NHL stars, such as Brian and Joey Mullen. Next, Francis went to St. Louis as president and general manager of the Blues. In 1982 he became the Hall's first and only NHL goalie elected as a Builder.

Paul Coffey, Ray Bourque and Larry Murphy

71 B. 2004

Three of the game's greatest blue-liners all retired in 2001, presenting the Hall of Fame with the unique opportunity to welcome the best defensive point-producers in a generation at one induction ceremony. The Hall embraced the occasion and themed its class of 2004 around Raymond Bourque, Paul Coffey and Larry Murphy, a trio of full-range rearguards who used their speed and skill in careers celebrated for scorecard consistency. All three men started in the NHL within a year of each other and played more than 20 seasons in the league. They combined for an awesome 4,326 points in 4,636 games, among the highest aggregates ever in a Hall class.

Players of the 2004 Hall of Fame Class

Inductee	Career	Regular Season		Playoffs		
		GP	Scoring	GP	Scoring	Cups
Ray Bourque	1979–2001	1612	410-1169-1579	214	41-139-180	1
Paul Coffey	1980–2001	1409	396-1135-1531	194	59-137-196	4
Larry Murphy	1980–2001	1615	287-929-1216	215	37-115-152	4

72 C. Mats Sundin of Sweden

When Mats Sundin was elected to the Hall of Fame in 2012, his induction meant much more than a celebration of his NHL career. While donning Toronto's blue and white, Sundin produced the league's first 500th goal by a Swede and became the club's all-time scoring leader, with 420 goals and 987 points. However, his play for Team Sweden at the World Championships and the Olympics marked his greatest success. Sundin won a trio of World titles, in 1991, 1992 and 1998, and captained Tre Kronor to a gold medal at the 2006 Olympics. Sundin's most memorable marker came as a 20-year-old before a world audience in 1991, when he furnished a spine-tingling coast-to-coast rush against the defending-champion Soviets and netted a 2–1 tie-breaker for the World Championship. He was the youngest player on either team. Selected first overall by Quebec in 1989, Sundin is the first European to secure the top draft position and the second Swede in the Hall, after Borje Salming's entry in 1996.

Mats Sundin: World-Class Center of the Hall of Fame

NHL Career Stats (1990–2009)					
Regular Season					
GP	Scoring	+/–	PIM	Shots	S%
1346	564-785-1349	73	1093	4015	14.0
Playoffs					
GP	Scoring	+/–	PIM	Shots	S%
91	38-44-82	2	74	246	15.4

International Career Stats (1990–2006)			
Competition	GP	Scoring	**Team Results**
World Junior Championship	7	5-2-7	Finished 5th
IIHF World Championship	35	18-26-44	Gold (3), Silver (2), Bronze (2)
World Cup of Hockey	8	5-8-13	Semi-finalists
Canada Cup	6	2-4-6	Finished 4th
Olympics	16	11-9-20	Gold (1)

In His Footsteps:
Hall of Fame Families

When Mark Howe was inducted in 2011, the Howes became just the 10th family with a father and son or brother act honored as Players in the Hall of Fame. The roots of this hallowed tradition trace back to Frank Patrick's 1950 induction, three years after his brother Lester's call. More than a decade later, the Hall welcomed its first two-generation clan, with the Seiberts. In this game, match the first name combinations with the correct family name and figure out the men's relationship. Score extra points if you know their induction years.

For solutions, turn the page.

Doug & Max

Lester & Lynn

Oliver & Earl

Frank & Georges

Gordie & Mark

Bobby & Brett

Maurice & Henri

Phil & Tony

Bill & Bun

Charlie & Lionel

Family	First Names	Relationship
Esposito		
	&	
Bentley		
	&	
Cook		
	&	
Hull		
	&	
Boucher		
	&	
Patrick		
	&	
Richard		
	&	
Seibert		
	&	
Conacher		
	&	
Howe		
	&	

In His Footsteps:
Hall of Fame Families
Solutions

Family	First Name	Induction Year	Relationship
Esposito	Phil	1984	Brothers
	& Tony	1988	
Bentley	Doug	1964	Brothers
	& Max	1966	
Cook	Bill	1952	Brothers
	& Bun	1995	
Hull	Bobby	1983	Father/Son
	& Brett	2009	
Boucher	Frank	1958	Brothers
	& George	1960	
Patrick	Lester	1947	Father/Son
	& Lynn	1980	
Richard	Maurice	1961	Brothers
	& Henri	1979	
Seibert	Oliver	1961	Father/Son
	& Earl	1963	
Conacher	Charlie	1961	Brothers
	& Lionel	1994	
Howe	Gordie	1972	Father/Son
	& Mark	2011	

Brothers Tony and Phil Esposito

Bobby Hull and Stan Mikita

The Game Breakers

The Golden Jet was the most electrifying offensive force in the NHL during the 1960s. High-flying Bobby Hull and his booming shot terrified goalies, many of whom were thankful when he moved to the rival WHA in 1972. Before his departure, Hull had scored 604 NHL goals in a 15-year span between 1957–58 and 1971–72 and compiled an unprecedented seven goal-scoring titles—one more than runner-up Phil Esposito, who collected six straight after Hull. In this chapter, we target some of the greatest NHL record-holders in the Hall of Fame.

73

Which Hall of Fame member owns the NHL record for the most consecutive games with a goal?

A.
Joe Malone of the Montreal Canadiens in 1917–18

B.
Punch Broadbent of the Ottawa Senators in 1921–22

C.
Wayne Gretzky of the Edmonton Oilers in 1984–85

D.
Mario Lemieux of the Pittsburgh Penguins in 1992–93

74

Martin Brodeur and Braden Holtby hold the NHL record for most wins in one season with 48, but which Hall of Famer shares Brodeur's combined league mark of 59 regular-season and playoff victories?

A.
Terry Sawchuk of the Detroit Red Wings

B.
Ken Dryden of the Montreal Canadiens

C.
Bernie Parent of the Philadelphia Flyers

D.
Patrick Roy of the Colorado Avalanche

75 Which Hall of Famer can claim the NHL's highest penalty-minute count by a Hart Trophy MVP?

A.	**B.**	**C.**	**D.**
Gordie Howe in 1951–52	Jean Béliveau in 1955–56	Bobby Clarke in 1974–75	Mark Messier in 1989–90

76 Who recorded his first 100 NHL goals the quickest?

A.
Mike Bossy of the
New York Islanders

B.
Brett Hull of the Calgary Flames
and St. Louis Blues

C.
Wayne Gretzky of the
Edmonton Oilers

D.
Future Hall candidate Teemu
Selanne of the Winnipeg Jets

Answers 73-74

73 B. Punch Broadbent of the Ottawa Senators in 1921–22

If old-time hockey had a tandem of the caliber of Wayne Gretzky and Jari Kurri, that duo was the Gold Dust Twins. Hall of Famers Cy Denneny and Punch Broadbent were the offensive backbone of hockey's first NHL dynasty, the Ottawa Senators, winners of four Stanley Cups (three with the twosome) during the 1920s. But for all their sparkling play, Denneny and Broadbent added grit to their game, keeping the opposition honest while racking up big points. In the 1921–22 four-team circuit, players quickly learned their opponents' weaknesses. The dynamic duo finished first and second in league scoring, as Broadbent struck pay dirt with a 32-14-46 record and a 27-goal rampage in 16 straight games between December and February. Not even Gretzky could do that.

Punch Broadbent's NHL Record Goal Streak

1921–22 Regular Season				
Game in Streak	Date	Rival	Score	Goals/Tally
1	Dec. 24	Montreal	10–0 W	1 / 1 of 27
2	Dec. 28	Montreal	2–1 W	1 / 2 of 27
3	Dec. 31	Hamilton	4–0 W	1 / 3 of 27
4	Jan. 4	Toronto	3–2 L	1 / 4 of 27
5	Jan. 7	Montreal	4–2 W	2 / 6 of 27
6	Jan. 11	Toronto	7–2 W	2 / 8 of 27
7	Jan. 14	Toronto	5–2 W	2 / 10 of 27
8	Jan. 18	Montreal	10–6 W	3 / 13 of 27
9	Jan. 21	Hamilton	7–6 L	3 / 16 of 27
10	Jan. 25	Hamilton	4–2 W	2 / 18 of 27
11	Jan. 28	Toronto	2–1 W	2 / 20 of 27
12	Feb. 1	Montreal	4–2 W	2 / 22 of 27
13	Feb. 4	Hamilton	10–6 W	1 / 23 of 27
14	Feb. 8	Hamilton	9–1 L	1 / 24 of 27
15	Feb. 11	Toronto	4–4 T	1 / 25 of 27
16	Feb. 15	Montreal	6–6 T	2 / 27 of 27

74 C. Bernie Parent of the Philadelphia Flyers

Evaluate a record by its longevity, and Bernie Parent's illustrious mark of 47 wins in 1973–74 is the goalie's gold standard. No stopper bested it for 33 years, until Martin Brodeur registered 48 victories in 2006–07 and, later, Braden Holtby did it with the same number in 2015–16. However, Parent equals Brodeur in combined playoff and regular-season totals in one year, each having an all-time NHL high of 59 triumphs. Holtby totaled 54. Brodeur chalked up 43 regular-season wins and another 16 in post-season play in 1999–2000, and Parent had a 47-12 win count in 1973–74. That season was sensational for Parent in the loss column too. He tied Terry Sawchuk's unofficial record for fewest defeats by a 70-game netminder, losing just 13 times with Philadelphia. Parent's 12 shutouts that year did not set a new mark, but after duplicating the total again in 1974–75, his two-year aggregate of 24 tied him with Sawchuk's modern-era mark for most shutouts in back-to-back seasons. Moreover, his crease work was the key to the Flyers' success. Philly's goon-squad tactics would not have won Stanley Cups in 1974 and 1975 if Parent had not been a wall. As a measure of his worth, the Flyers retired Parent's No. 1—a goalie first in the NHL—in October 1979, five years before his Hall entry.

75 B. Jean Béliveau in 1955–56

A gentleman throughout his life and his career, Jean Béliveau may be the most unlikely MVP to lead Hart Trophy winners in box time. On a team with no designated policeman to protect skill players, Béliveau spared no quarter to prove himself as a sophomore. While blossoming into a scoring champion in 1955–56 with a league-leading 47 goals and 88 points, he was assessed an MVP-record 143 minutes for battling mugging rivals. It was his most-penalized season—a year that demonstrated his unique blend of skill, grit, elegance and an intuitive feel for the game, which quickly earned him league-wide respect. Béliveau won 10 Stanley Cups with Montreal, five as team captain. He was inducted into the Hall immediately after his retirement in 1972.

The Hall of Fame's Hard-Hitting Hart Winners

Player	Induction Year	Team	Season	Scoring	PIM
Jean Béliveau	1972	Montreal	1955–56	47-41-88	143
Bobby Clarke	1987	Philadelphia	1975–76	30-89-119	136
Bobby Clarke	1987	Philadelphia	1974–75	27-89-116	125
Bobby Orr	1979	Boston	1969–70	33-87-120	125
Nels Stewart	1952	Mtl. Maroons	1925–26	34-8-42	119
Bobby Orr	1979	Boston	1971–72	37-80-117	106
Eddie Shore	1947	Boston	1932–33	8-27-35	102

76 A. Mike Bossy of the New York Islanders

Mike Bossy's great misfortune in a near-perfect career was his timing. He suffered the fate of playing opposite Wayne Gretzky and Guy Lafleur during their peak years, and as a result he never won an NHL scoring title despite his off-the-radar totals. Still, he set a few league records, including the quickest 100 goals from the start of a career. In his freshman season of 1977–78, he scored 53 times, making him the first rookie to crack the 50-goal plateau. When he recorded his 47th goal of 1978–79 on February 19, he also tallied his 100th career goal. It was Bossy's 129th NHL game. He had broken Maurice Richard's mark of 100 goals in 134 games. Future Hall of Famer Teemu Selanne hit the 100-goal mark in one more match than Bossy, at 130. Gretzky needed 145 games, which is a good indication of Bossy's skill level.

77 Which Hall of Fame inductee was the first NHL defenseman to score 500 points?

A.
Doug Harvey of the Montreal Canadiens

B.
Babe Pratt of the Toronto Maple Leafs

C.
Bobby Orr of the Boston Bruins

D.
Bill Gadsby of the Detroit Red Wings

 78 Hall of Famer Maurice Richard's long-standing NHL record for most overtime playoff goals was broken by which other Hall of Famer?

A.
Frank Mahovlich

B.
Stan Mikita

C.
Glenn Anderson

D.
Joe Sakic

79 Which Hall of Fame goalie netted the most shutouts in one NHL season?

A.
George
Hainsworth
of the Montreal
Canadiens

B.
Roy Worters
of the Pittsburgh
Pirates

C.
Glenn Hall
of the Chicago
Black Hawks

D.
Billy Smith
of the New York
Islanders

80 Which NHL defenseman most recently recorded 100 points and became a top-10 scoring leader?

A.
Denis Potvin
of the New York
Islanders

B.
Ray Bourque
of the Boston
Bruins

C.
Brian Leetch
of the New York
Rangers

D.
Paul Coffey
of the Pittsburgh
Penguins

77 D. Bill Gadsby of the Detroit Red Wings

Bill Gadsby (No. 4) is among a small contingent of NHLers in the Hall of Fame who never won the Stanley Cup or an individual trophy. A superb two-way defenseman, equally skilled as a shot blocker, puck rusher and playmaker, Gadsby anchored his teams with a tireless work ethic for 20 seasons. In 1965–66 he became the first NHLer to play 300 or more games with three different clubs—a tribute to his value with Chicago, New York and Detroit. However, Gadsby's three Norris Trophy nominations ended in frustration, and when he finally played for a contender in Detroit, the Red Wings lost three Cup finals before his retirement in 1966. "You can't dwell on the disappoint-ment," Gadsby once said. "I had a wonderful career and got to play with some great players." Gadsby recorded the league's first 500th point by a rearguard in his 17th season, on November 4, 1962, just three months ahead of Doug Harvey's 500th, in February 1963.

78 D. Joe Sakic

The story of Maurice Richard was always about more than a great player. His prolific scoring skills and fiery play made the game modern in almost every significant way and became a battle standard that inspired nationalistic fervor in the hockey hotbed of Quebec. Few equaled his passion, bravery or famous competitive edge. Fewer still could match his box-score records, which were only surpassed with the advent of longer schedules. Richard's six postseason overtime goals, his most resilient mark, lasted nearly a half-century of NHL play and was only broken by 2012 Hall inductee Joe Sakic, who dethroned hockey's best clutch performer during the 2006 playoffs. Sakic topped Richard's record by scoring his seventh career OT winner against Dallas and then locked up the mark for years to come with another in 2008 versus Minnesota, his eighth extra-period postseason tally. Sakic won two Stanley Cups with Colorado, in 1996 and 2001. He led playoff scoring both times and was named MVP in 1996.

The Clutch Performers:
Most Career Overtime Playoff Goals

Player	Induction Year	Team(s)	Goals	Rivals in Series
Joe Sakic	2012	Colorado	8	Van., 1996 CQF; Chi., 1996 CSF; Edm., 1998 CQF; St. L., 2001 CF; S.J., 2004 CSF; S.J., 2004 CSF; Dal., 2006 CQF; Min., 2008 CQF
Maurice Richard	1961	Montreal	6	Bos., 1946 F; Det., 1951 SF; Det., 1951 SF; Tor., 1951 F; NYR, 1957 SF; Bos., 1958 F
Glenn Anderson	2008	Edmonton, Toronto, St. Louis	5	LA, 1985 DSF; Cgy., 1986 DF; Wpg., 1987 DF; LA, 1993 CF; Tor., 1996 CQF

Note: Several players have four overtime playoff goals

79 A. George Hainsworth of the Montreal Canadiens

While modern goalies populate much of the NHL record books, a few old-timers, such as George Hainsworth, have stubbornly held onto their place in history. Hainsworth wasn't flashy and his repertoire included few acrobatic moves, yet he put up the highest number of zeroes in one season, posting 22 shutouts in 1928–29. Admittedly, it was the final season before forward passing was allowed in all three zones, and the 44-game schedule produced a league-wide average of fewer than three goals per game—the lowest average in NHL action ever. Even so, Hainsworth led all starters in the 10-team NHL, yielding only 43 goals for a microscopic 0.92 goals-against average. He played another eight seasons and retired with a league-high 94 shutouts, the all-time third best total behind Martin Brodeur and Terry Sawchuk.

80 C. Brian Leetch of the New York Rangers

While Paul Coffey remains the last rearguard to crack the NHL's top 10, his seventh-place finish came with a 14-44-58 record in the lockout-shortened 1994–95 season. The last time a top-10 player had scored 100 points manning the blue line was in 1991–92, when Brian Leetch collected 102 points for ninth overall, 29 points behind league-leader Mario Lemieux. Leetch was explosively mobile and knew where to pinch to create scoring chances. He collected 22 goals and 80 assists to become only the fifth blue-liner to own a top-10 position with 100 points or more. Not all top-10 defensemen needed 100 points to get there. Erik Karlsson tied for 10th overall with a 78-point season in 2011–12, Ray Bourque finished 1986–87 in 10th spot on 95 points and Red Kelly had top-10s with 54, 49 and 46 points during the early 1950s. Multiple rearguards cracking the top-10 in one season is rare; the last occasion came in 1973–74, with Bobby Orr and Brad Park.

Hall of Fame Rearguards with 100-Point Seasons

Player	Induction Year	Team	Season	Scoring	Position	Points Behind Leader
Bobby Orr	1979	Boston	1969–70	33-87-120*	1st	0
Denis Potvin	1991	NY Islanders	1978–79	31-70-101	7th	33
Al MacInnis	2007	Calgary	1990–91	28-75-103	9th	60
Paul Coffey	2004	Edmonton	1983–84	40-86-126*	2nd	79
Brian Leetch	2009	NY Rangers	1991–92	22-80-102	9th	29

*1st of multiple 100-point seasons. Orr had six and Coffey had five.

81 The NHL's fastest game-winning goal came off the stick of which Hall of Fame sniper?

A.
Charlie Conacher of the Toronto Maple Leafs

B.
Bobby Hull of the Chicago Black Hawks

C.
Phil Esposito of the Boston Bruins

D.
Bernie Geoffrion of the Montreal Canadiens

82 Who owns the longest consecutive point-scoring streak in NHL playoff history?

A.
Al MacInnis of the Calgary Flames

B.
Serge Savard of the Montreal Canadiens

C.
Reggie Leach of the Philadelphia Flyers

D.
Bryan Trottier of the New York Islanders

83 The longest shutout sequence in NHL history was recorded by which Hall of Fame goalie?

A.
Glenn Hall
of the Chicago
Black Hawks

B.
Alex Connell
of the Ottawa
Senators

C.
Johnny Bower
of the Toronto
Maple Leafs

D.
Patrick Roy
of the Colorado
Avalanche

84 Who owns the NHL record for most goals in a calendar month?

A.
Bryan Trottier
of the
New York
Islanders

B.
Eric Lindros
of the
Philadelphia
Flyers

C.
Teemu Selanne
of the
Winnipeg Jets

D.
Sergei Makarov
of the
Calgary Flames

81 A. Charlie Conacher of the Toronto Maple Leafs

One of old-time hockey's least-known trivia facts comes courtesy of that era's greatest star, Charlie Conacher. According to press reports of the February 6, 1932, game, the Maple Leafs crowd had hardly settled into their seats when Conacher was "handed the puck by Busher Jackson from the opening faceoff and let loose a whistling drive from near the blue line that found the top corner of the net" behind Boston's Wilf Cude. Although others such as Bryan Trottier and Alexander Mogilny have netted faster goals from the opening faceoff, none have been game winners. Perhaps Trottier and Mogilny needed a Lorne Chabot between the pipes. After Conacher's goal at 0:07 of the first period, Chabot preserved the early winner by stoning the Bruins with 30 saves through 59:53 minutes in Toronto's 6–0 blowout.

82 D. Bryan Trottier of the New York Islanders

It's the kind of playoff record that defines a career. It may also be the best reason why Bryan Trottier won Hall approval in his first year of eligibility. In his prime, few teams could contain the hard-driving center. He won a rec room of silverware, including rookie of the year honors, regular-season and postseason scoring titles and MVP awards. But when he strung together a 27-game point-scoring streak between 1980 and 1982, it set a standard approached by no other player, including Hall members Wayne Gretzky and Al MacInnis, who each managed 19-game runs. "He had nice soft hands but he could also knock over a moose," said former Islanders GM Bill Torrey. A host of talented performers contributed to New York's championships in the 1980s, but none played a larger role in the club's success than Trottier. Part scoring ace and part inspirational leader, Trottier bagged 42 points in those 27 games, but he was most dominant during the 1981 playoffs, when he pegged a point in all 18 games the Islanders played, establishing the postseason's longest point-scoring streak.

Bryan Trottier: Titan of the Postseason

The NHL's Longest Playoff Point-Scoring Streak: 1980–1982					
27-Game Record Streak				**Year Totals**	
Season	**GP**	**Scoring**	**Rivals in Series**	**GP**	**Scoring**
1980	7	3-5-8	Buffalo, SF; Philadelphia, F	21	12-17-29
1981*	18	11-18-29	Toronto, PR; Edmonton, QF; NY Rangers, SF; Minnesota, F	18	11-18-29
1982	2	2-3-5	Pittsburgh, DSF	19	6-23-29
Total	**27**	**16-26-42**			

*Single playoff-year record of 18 games

83 B. Alex Connell of the Ottawa Senators

Although Alex Connell only led the NHL in goals-against average once during his 12 years, he established netminding numbers that remain unchallenged today. Connell stopped rubber during the original dead-puck era, before forward passing was permitted in 1929. The previous rule proved to be a league-wide offense killer, and while most goalies benefitted from its stifling play, it is Connell who owns the NHL's all-time best career average of 1.91. However, his most prominent record remains a shutout sequence of 460 minutes and 49 seconds. Among modern goalies, only Brian Boucher has come close, with his out-of-nowhere string of five blanks in 2003–04. Still, Boucher fell short of Connell's number by 128 minutes and 48 seconds—more than two complete games. Connell's celebrated stretch came in 1927–28's 44-game schedule, when he posted 15 shutouts with eight wins and seven scoreless ties. Three of those draws, which included overtimes, were part of his monster six-game shutout run.

Six Games of Perfection: Hockey's Greatest Shutout Sequence

Alex Connell's 1927–28 Streak Stats			
Date	Rival	Score	Shutout time
Jan. 28	Montreal	2–1 W	25:39
Jan. 31	Toronto	4–0 W	60:00
Feb. 2	Mtl. Maroons	1–0 W	69:20
Feb. 7	NY Rangers	0–0 T	70:00
Feb. 9	NY Rangers	0–0 T	70:00
Feb. 16	Pittsburgh	0–0 T	70:00
Feb. 18	Montreal	1–0 W	60:00
Feb. 22	Chicago	3–2 W	35:50

84 C. Teemu Selanne of the Winnipeg Jets

Statistics, awards and a championship demonstrate the offensive brilliance and stamina of Teemu Selanne's 21-year NHL career. However, it is what he did as a rookie with Winnipeg in 1992–93 that still reverberates in record books today. The Jets' marksman cranked out the league's hottest scoring month ever in March 1993, after firing a record 20 goals in 14 games, including five power-play goals, two hat tricks, two game winners, one penalty-shot goal and one empty-net goal. Early in the month, on March 2, he had registered his 54th goal, breaking Mike Bossy's rookie mark. Three weeks later, on March 23, he smashed Peter Stastny's 109-point freshman record. Selanne finished his NHL apprenticeship sharing the overall league lead with 76 goals, which obliterated Bossy's total by a dizzying 23 goals. Selanne had become the "Finnish Flash." He never tallied a better season in his 684-goal career.

85 Which Hall of Famer was the first European-trained player to compile 1,000 NHL points?

A.
Borje Salming of Sweden

B.
Jari Kurri of Finland

C.
Peter Stastny of Czechoslovakia

D.
Pavel Bure of the USSR

86 Who set a modern-era NHL shutout record in his rookie season?

A.
Jacques Plante of the Montreal Canadiens

B.
Terry Sawchuk of the Detroit Red Wings

C.
Tony Esposito of the Chicago Black Hawks

D.
Grant Fuhr of the Edmonton Oilers

87 Which Hall of Famer owns the unofficial NHL record for being crowned regular-season penalty leader most often during his career?

A.
Pierre Pilote

B.
Red Horner

C.
Eddie Shore

D.
Ted Lindsay

88 Which modern-day player entered the Hall of Fame having scored the highest percentage of his team's total goals in one season?

A.
Pavel Bure of the
Florida Panthers

B.
Wayne Gretzky
of the Edmonton
Oilers

C.
Denis Savard
of the Chicago
Blackhawks

D.
Brett Hull of the
St. Louis Blues

85 C. Peter Stastny of Czechoslovakia

Peter Stastny was the European Wayne Gretzky, with an elite skill set that would earn him the NHL's second-highest point total during the 1980s, behind only the Great One himself. Already an international star at the time of his defection from Czechoslovakia in 1980, the 24-year-old Stastny set a torrid scoring pace in NHL play, rattling off six consecutive 100-point seasons for the Quebec Nordiques. Before the decade ended, he was the first non-North American to score 1,000 NHL points, a distinction that came in October 1989, just months ahead of Finnish sniper Jari Kurri's millennium marker. But Stastny's greatest impact on the North American game went beyond score sheets. His dramatic escape created headlines around the world and forced Eastern Bloc nations to reconsider their hard-line policies for veteran stars. Almost at once, an NHL job seemed possible for hundreds of Europeans—the next wave of change that altered NHL hockey forever. Stastny won Hall credentials in 1998.

86 C. Tony Esposito of the Chicago Black Hawks

Only one modern goalie broke into the exclusive ranks of zero heroes George Hainsworth, Alex Connell and Hal Winkler. It happened in 1969–70, when Chicago's Tony Esposito shut out opponents 15 times to equal the four-decade-old total of Connell and Winkler, earning himself a second-place tie behind Hainsworth's impenetrable record of 22 blanks, set in 1928–29. Unlike the old-timers, "Tony O" played an unorthodox butterfly style that allowed him to cover the lower half of the net when he went down. "I stopped a lot of pucks without seeing them," admitted Esposito. Opponents also had trouble with his catching glove. A lefty, he caught with his right hand, so the glove was in the opposite spot to where shooters normally expected it. Remarkably, Esposito posted a shutout almost every fourth start in 1969–70.

Tony O's Year of Zeroes

1969–70 Regular-Season Stats					15 Shutouts Stats		
GP	Record	GA	GAA	Min	GA	SA	SV
63	38-17-8	136	2.17	3763	0	428	428

Honors: Calder, Vezina, 1st All-Star, Hart runner-up

15 Shutouts Scorecard							
Date	Rival	Score	Saves	Date	Rival	Score	Saves
Oct. 25	Montreal	5–0	30	Jan. 14	Pittsburgh	5–0	28
Nov. 9	Toronto	9–0	23	Jan. 17	Boston	1–0	36
Nov. 16	Montreal	1–0	29	Jan. 31	Philadelphia	5–0	34
Nov. 26	Los Angeles	6–0	33	Mar. 11	Boston	0–0*	24
Dec. 19	Oakland	4–0	23	Mar. 22	St. Louis	1–0	21
Dec. 21	St. Louis	4–0	22	Mar. 26	Detroit	1–0	35
Dec. 27	Pittsburgh	3–0	30	Mar. 29	Toronto	4–0	35
Jan. 7	Detroit	7–0	25	*Scoreless tie			

87 B. Red Horner

A few heavyweights have been promoted to hockey's highest individual honor as a Hall member, but not many are in the weight class of Red Horner. Remembered as the "bad boy" of hockey, Horner led the NHL in penalty minutes a record five consecutive seasons and held the title seven times during a 12-year fight-filled career. Unlike other tough guys who ultimately made it into the Hall based on their game skills, Horner's chief talent was rocking the opposition into submission with devastating hits. Meanwhile, it didn't hurt that he played for Toronto's influential Conn Smythe, who petitioned the selection committee with this: "I would venture to state that his [Horner] penalties never hurt us at any time ... Of all the great body checkers there have been in the National Hockey League, no one hit a man fairer or harder than Red Horner." Smythe's glowing support won the day, and Horner entered the Hall with a career 1,254 penalty minutes in 490 games. He potted 42 goals and 110 assists—among the lowest career totals by an NHL regular in the Hall—but his Maple Leafs went to the Stanley Cup Final on seven occasions. They won just once, in 1932, turning Horner's palooka image into a prize-fighting Cup champion.

88 A. Pavel Bure of the Florida Panthers

It was only a matter of time before the Hall of Fame issued landing clearance to the Russian Rocket. Pavel Bure may have been an enigma, and sometimes a prima donna, but he was also a goal-scoring wizard, built by the Soviet hockey system of the once-invincible "Big Red Machine" and its weave-and-pass style of play based on speed, agility and puck control. Before calling it quits in 2005 due to complications from a chronically injured knee, Bure had amassed 437 goals and 779 points in 702 games, a career average of better than a point per game. His breakaway pace and virtuosity with the puck generated five 50-goal seasons, including two with the Florida Panthers, where he set 21 club records in almost every offensive category. However, the Panthers' experiment with Bure ultimately failed, and the lunch-pail team couldn't find the manpower to complement his finesse game. As a consequence, Bure scored an NHL record 29.5 percent of Florida's goals, blasting home 59 of the team's 200 goals in 2000–01. The Russian Rocket joined the Hall in 2012, four years after his eligibility.

89 Which Hall member became the first rearguard to reach the 1,000-point plateau in NHL play?

A.
Paul Coffey of the Pittsburgh Penguins

B.
Bobby Orr of the Boston Bruins

C.
Larry Robinson of the Montreal Canadiens

D.
Denis Potvin of the New York Islanders

90 For what feat is Hall of Famer Bill Mosienko famous?

A. Mosienko recorded the most shots on goal by an NHL rookie

B. Mosienko scored the NHL's fastest hat trick

C. Mosienko set the NHL mark for most consecutive games played

D. Mosienko scored the most goals in one NHL game

91 Who registered the highest percentage of his team's total offense in an NHL season of 70 or more games?

A.
Pat LaFontaine of the Buffalo Sabres

B.
Wayne Gretzky of the Edmonton Oilers

C.
Mario Lemieux of the Pittsburgh Penguins

D.
Pavel Bure of the Florida Panthers

92 Which Hall of Famer has participated in the most combined NHL games as a player and coach?

A.
Jacques Lemaire

C.
Larry Robinson

B.
Red Kelly

D.
Al Arbour

89 D. Denis Potvin of the New York Islanders

Denis Potvin won four consecutive Stanley Cups as captain of the New York Islanders, but his Hall nomination was "the ring of all rings," according to the defensive stalwart. During his 15-year tour de force he played in nine All-Star Games, collected three Norris Trophies and scored 1,052 points. His breakthrough point came on a deflected goal against Buffalo in April 1987. Potvin netted the league milestone on 290 goals and 710 assists. Three years later, Paul Coffey repeated the feat with the league's second 1,000th point by a rearguard. Neither Bobby Orr nor Larry Robinson ever did it: Orr had 915 points and Robinson 958.

90 B. Mosienko scored the NHL's fastest hat trick

On March 23, 1952, Chicago's Bill Mosienko stepped onto the ice against the New York Rangers, and in 21 seconds of play he produced the defining moment of his 711-game NHL career. Nothing else during his 14 years of hockey is better known than what happened at 6:09, 6:20 and 6:30 of the third period against New York's Lorne Anderson. Mosienko's three goals that night remain the league's fastest hat trick, although his less-familiar feats are what made him Hall of Fame material. He set the bar high as a rookie in 1943–44, scoring 70 points—a freshman record that stood until Gilbert Perreault topped it 27 years later. Mosienko lined up with Doug Bentley and Clint Smith, the very first trio to break the 200-point mark in one season, with 219. Later, Mosienko teamed with brothers Doug and Max Bentley to form Chicago's legendary Pony Line. Max and Doug earned multiple scoring titles, while Mosienko took home his only award, the Lady Byng Trophy as most gentlemanly player, in 1945. Mosienko notched 54 points without a single penalty that year, still a league points record by an unpenalized player. The threesome was inducted in successive years, Doug in 1964, Mosienko in 1965 and Max in 1966.

Hockey's Hottest Hat Trick

March 23, 1952
Madison Square Garden
Chicago 7, New York 6

First Period

1, Chicago, Bodnar 14 (Gadsby, Mosienko), :44.

2, New York, Eddolls 3, 4:50.

3, New York, Raleigh 19 (Stewart, Stanley), 17:12.

4, New York, Slowinski 20 (Raleigh, Stewart), 18:35.

5, Chicago, Horeck 9 (Hucul, Finney), 18:47.

Penalties: None

Second Period

6, New York, Stewart 15 (Slowinski), 13:19.

7, New York, Dickenson 14 (Hergesheimer, Ronty), 15:55.

Penalties: None

Third Period

8, New York, Slowinski 21 (Raleigh), 3:37.

9, Chicago, Mosienko 29 (Bodnar), 6:09.

10, Chicago, Mosienko 30 (Bodnar), 6:20.

11, Chicago, Mosienko 31 (Bodnar), 6:30.

12, Chicago, Finney 5 (Hucul, Fogolin), 13:50.

13, Chicago, Finney 6 (Gadsby), 19:22.

Penalties: None

Goaltenders	Time	GA	ENG	DEC
Chicago, Lumley	60:00	6	0	W
New York, Anderson	60:00	7	0	L

165

91 C. Mario Lemieux of the Pittsburgh Penguins

Blessed with the offensive genius of Mario Lemieux and cursed by the lackluster support around him, Pittsburgh failed to gain a playoff berth in 1987–88, a building year for a franchise struggling in a very tough Patrick Division race. Lemieux's stratospheric numbers set NHL records in futility: He held the most goals (70) and the most points (168) by a player on a non-playoff team. A year later, in 1988–89, the Penguins ranked third behind Calgary and Los Angeles in offense, with 347 goals, due largely to No. 66, who figured in on 199 of them, with 85 goals and 114 assists. Lemieux's 57.3 percent remains the highest percentage of a team's total offense by a player in a season of 70 games or more.

92 D. Al Arbour

The longevity of Al Arbour's NHL career is Gordie-Howesque. In a six-decade run from 1953–54 to 2007–08, Arbour combined his stay-at-home defenseman roll and his bench acumen to amass a record 2,528 matches, including playoff contests in which he played on four Stanley Cup winners and coached another four on Long Island. The move behind the bench happened immediately after his retirement in early 1970–71. He ran St. Louis for the balance of the season and part of the next year before his career moved to the Islanders. His regular-season and playoff totals as a bench boss rival only Scotty Bowman's: Arbour has 1,816 games to Bowman's 2,494. With a respectful nod to Scotty's and Gordie's numbers (1,924 NHL matches), no other player or coach, inductee or non-Hall member, has broken Arbour's 2,528–NHL game benchmark. He was inducted into the Hall in 1996.

The 2,000-Game Club:
The Hall's Top NHL Player-Turned-Coaches

Player	Induction Year	Career	Player GP		Coach GC		Total Games	Cups
			RS	PS	RS	PS		
Al Arbour	1996	1953–2008	626	86	1607	209	2528	8
Jacques Lemaire	1984	1967–2011	853	145	1262	117	2377	9
Red Kelly	1969	1947–1977	1316	164	742	62	2284	8
Pat Quinn	2016	1968–2010	606	11	1400	183	2200	0
Larry Robinson	1995	1972–2006	1384	227	501	52	2164	7
Bob Pulford	1991	1956–2000	1079	89	829	71	2068	4

Note: A few other player-turned-coaches, such as Joel Quenneville and Lindy Ruff, have accrued more than 2000 NHL games, but none is a Hall member to date.

Spoken from the Heart

Little in training prepares an athlete for that unfamiliar step to the podium to accept Hall recognition. It is a ceremony of validation, dedicated parents, coaches and teammates, hockey dreams and life lessons. Most importantly, it's about finding one's place and purpose among the game's pantheon of greats, an ideal expressed in 2001 by Mike Gartner: "As I look up at the men on this wall whose images ... are looking down at me with measuring eyes, I only hope I can stand tall with you." Match the player inductee and induction quote.

For solutions, turn the page.

Ray Bourque

Mats Sundin

Brett Hull

Clark Gillies

Pat LaFontaine

Larry Murphy

Mark Messier

1. [_____] "As players, we were smart enough to realize that if we just somehow found a way to support Wayne [Gretzky], that eventually his career was destined for a Stanley Cup. And if we could find a way to support him, ultimately, we would ride his coattails to a Stanley Cup."

2. [_____] "My father, you gave me giant footsteps to follow. You taught me to speak my mind. And you gave me the best advice in your own unique way ... And I quote: 'The further you are from the play the closest you are to it.' And I am really fortunate that I was able to figure out what the hell he was talking about."

3. [_____] "Believe it or not I played with 313 different teammates in the NHL. I played 757 games with Don Sweeney and that was the most by far. But I also played one game with 12 different guys and I want to thank all of you, because you are what made it special."

4. [_____] "Many coaches claim there is no "I" in the word team. But Pat Quinn always claimed the opposite. As an individual you are responsible for your own work, your own development as a player. Don't hide behind the group or look at someone else to get the job done. So I agree Pat, there is an "I" in team. And that mentality helped me develop as a player and take responsibility for my own game."

5. [_____] "It was the night of my 15th birthday, February 22, 1980, when Mike Eruzione scored that famous goal when the U.S. team beat the Russians. And I heard Al Michaels saying, 'Do you believe in Miracles?' and at that point in my career I started to believe that maybe there was a chance I could play in the NHL."

6. [_____] "You don't get here by yourself. I was fortunate to play with two great linemates: Bryan Trottier and Mike Bossy ... It makes me very proud to have been part of what may have been one of the greatest hockey teams ever assembled."

7. [_____] "As a boy growing up in Scarborough I never dreamed as big as the Hockey Hall of Fame. But I did dream of playing in the NHL. I spent countless hours at home in our backyard with my friends playing for the Leafs and winning hundreds of Stanley Cups."

Spoken from the Heart
Solutions

1. Mark Messier: "As players, we were smart enough to realize that if we just somehow found a way to support Wayne [Gretzky], that eventually his career was destined for a Stanley Cup ... "

2. Brett Hull: "My father, you gave me giant footsteps to follow. You taught me to speak my mind. And you gave me the best advice in your own unique way ... And I quote: 'The further you are from the play the closest you are to it' ... "

3. Ray Bourque: "Believe it or not I played with 313 different teammates in the NHL. I played 757 games with Don Sweeney and that was the most by far ... "

4. Mats Sundin: "Many coaches claim there is no "I" in the word team. But Pat Quinn always claimed the opposite. As an individual you are responsible for your own work, your own development as a player ... "

5. Pat LaFontaine: "It was the night of my 15th birthday, February 22, 1980, when Mike Eruzione scored that famous goal when the U.S. team beat the Russians. And I heard Al Michaels saying, 'Do you believe in Miracles?' ... "

6. Clark Gillies: "You don't get here by yourself. I was fortunate to play with two great linemates: Bryan Trottier and Mike Bossy ... "

7. Larry Murphy: "As a boy growing up in Scarborough I never dreamed as big as the Hockey Hall of Fame. But I did dream of playing in the NHL ... "

Mats Sundin

Herb Cain

True
or False?

Every NHL scoring champion went on to become a Hall of Famer. True or false? The answer is false, thanks to Herb Cain, hockey's only eligible NHL scoring leader not honored in the Hall. It's definitely an oddity. But still consistent with Cain's rep as an outsider. Even after his 82-point season in 1943–44 smashed league records and set new marks that went unbeaten for years, he wasn't awarded a First All-Star Team berth at left wing that year. His black-sheep label is undeserved, especially considering he won two Stanley Cups and registered 400 career points, a total that is greater than 10 scoring champs who are in the Hall.

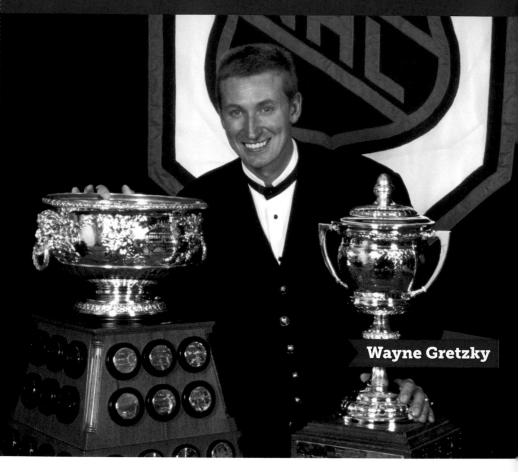

Wayne Gretzky

93 Wayne Gretzky was the only player inducted into the Hall of Fame in 1999. True or false?

94 While a few rookies have come close, the only freshman to win an NHL scoring title is a Hall of Famer from the 1920s. True or false?

95 Gordie Howe was the first Hall of Famer to participate in an NHL game (after gaining Hall membership). True or false?

96 An NHL player suspended for gambling during his career went on to the Hall of Fame, where he remains a member today. True or false?

Gordie Howe

Wayne Gretzky

93 True

Wayne Gretzky frequently reminded hockey fans that no one player is bigger than the game. Given everything Gretzky did, both as a record-setter on ice and as the consummate promoter off it, no one was more qualified to establish game code. Still, if any player transcended the sport, it was the Great One. He had the kind of career no one thought possible. And no one will ever duplicate it, not only because of the mass of records he smashed but because of how they were smashed. Further, his move to Los Angeles quite literally changed the playing field of North American hockey by popularizing the game in southern U.S. markets. However, his most important contribution was passion. During his Hall induction speech, No. 99 said: "What I think I did do is I paved the way for a lot of other people in the sense that I was told that I was not big enough, and maybe not fast enough or not strong enough, and I'm probably someone kids can look to and say, 'Well, he made it. Maybe I can make it.'" Gretzky was inducted immediately after his retirement and was the sole Player honoree of 1999.

94 True

Nels Stewart accomplished more during his first NHL season than many stars achieve in a lifetime of playing the game. He was that good as a rookie. Similar to Teemu Selanne's spectacular start with Winnipeg in 1992–93, Stewart joined the NHL at age 22 after several years of perfecting his game—in his case, with Cleveland of the United States Amateur Hockey Association. At 6-foot-1 and 195 pounds, Stewart was a towering presence in his era. He shot fast and played tough, copping 1925–26's NHL scoring title with 42 points and second-place in box time with 119 brutal minutes. Of the Montreal Maroons' 91 goals during his rookie campaign, Stewart had 34, a stunning 37 percent share. If a rookie award had existed in his day, Stewart would have won it, much as Selanne did in his first year, when he netted almost 24 percent of the Jets' total output. But Stewart did get the Hart Trophy and accounted for six of Montreal's 10 playoff goals against Victoria, turning the sophomore Maroons into the Stanley Cup champions of 1926. He retired in 1940 with 324 goals, a league record broken by Maurice Richard in 1952, the same year as Stewart's induction into the Hall.

Nels Stewart

Stewart vs. Selanne: Battle of the Young Guns

Nels Stewart, 1925–26 Montreal Maroons							
GP	Scoring	Per Game			Team GF	League Avg.*	% Team Goals
		G	A	P			
36	34-8-42	0.94	0.22	1.17	91	83	37.4
Teemu Selanne, 1992–93 Winnipeg Jets							
GP	Scoring	Per Game			Team GF	League Avg.*	% Team Goals
		G	A	P			
84	76-56-132	0.90	0.67	1.57	322	305	23.6

*League average of goals per team

95 False

While Gordie Howe is often credited as the first Hall member to lace up after induction, his landmark NHL return in 1979 wasn't the first in league history. That precedent was set by Hall of Fame referee Frank Udvari, who came out of the stands and more than a decade of retirement to replace injured referee Dave Newell during a New York Islanders–Atlanta Flames game on December 30, 1978—10 months before Howe's NHL comeback. "I don't know why I decided to do it," confessed Udvari. "I was 55 at the time and hadn't worked a game in 13 years. But the players made it easy for me to keep up." Udvari, supervisor of NHL officials, borrowed a pair of skates, courtesy of Islanders star Bryan Trottier, and donned the striped sweater one more time, whistling just two minor penalties and a disallowed goal, ironically scored by Trottier.

Frank Udvari

96 True

Babe Pratt belongs to that rare class of elite defensemen recognized for his scoring sorties up ice: the rushing rearguard. He could play the blue line effortlessly, but his offensive numbers spoke of a special skill set, best exhibited during his MVP record-setting 57-point season with Toronto in 1943–44. Later, his big-rush reputation was cemented when the Maple Leafs—a team that finished 28 points back of first place—made it to Game 7 of the Stanley Cup final and Pratt rushed and scored a third-period 2–1 tie-breaker to win the 1945 Cup. Unfortunately, Pratt's winning ways lost their luster less than a year later, in January 1946, when the NHL singled him out for gambling on hockey. Pratt, not unlike others in the game, bet frequently and allegedly on his Maple Leafs. The popular 12-year veteran was more expendable than other stars, and he paid the price: lifetime banishment. Sixteen days later, after a full confession and a promise to quit betting, Pratt was duly reinstated. He missed only five games (and not nine, as most records claim). However, the damage was done. He was soon dealt to Boston for a minor-leaguer and cash, which was quickly followed by another trade down to the AHL, again for cash. Twenty years after Pratt's fall from grace, he got his real pardon: Hall acceptance in 1966.

Babe Pratt

Gump Worsley

97 Hall of Fame goalie Gump Worsley holds the NHL record for most career losses. True or false?

98 The first NHL defenseman to notch a 20-goal season is not in the Hall of Fame. True or false?

99 Hall inductee Eric Lindros (2016) is the NHL's youngest Hart Trophy winner as regular-season MVP in league history. True or false?

100 No team has ever selected consecutive future Hall of Famers in the first two rounds of an NHL draft. True or false?

Harry Watson

97 False

Gump Worsley seemed destined for greatness. Even before his NHL career kicked into high gear, he had won a mitt full of awards while bouncing between five pro circuits, but all that changed with the New York Rangers. Tending twine for the Blueshirts became a protracted exercise in masochism for Worsley as the losses piled up, 271 in 10 seasons, including his last Rangers year, 1962–63, when the nightly shelling through 67 matches averaged 38.3 shots. Fortunately, the Gumper's trade to Montreal revived his career and sanity. He captured four Stanley Cups, and in his 11 years between the Canadiens and Minnesota North Stars he was beaten just another 81 times to become the NHL's first goalie to lose 300 games and win 300 games. Inducted into the Hall in 1980, Worsley owned a league-high 352 defeats and held that rank of wretchedness another three decades, until 2011–12, when a new all-time losses king was crowned with 371—future Hall candidate Martin Brodeur.

Martin Brodeur

98 True

In the era of stay-at-home defensemen, Flash Hollett excelled in both setting up plays and goal production. He developed his superb rushing and puck skills under the guidance of Boston greats Eddie Shore and Dit Clapper, ripping a record-high pair of 19-goal seasons with the Bruins during the early 1940s. But his best year came later, alongside Earl Seibert of Detroit in 1944–45, when he staged the NHL's first 20-goal performance by a blue-liner. Shore, Clapper and Seibert all became Hall of Famers, but unfortunately Hollett did not, the only rearguard in NHL history to post a 20-goal season before Bobby Orr scored 21 times a quarter century later, in 1968–69.

Flash Hollett

Answers 99-100

99 False

In a career highlighted by controversies and cut short by concussions, Lindros never did live up to the gargantuan expectations heaped on him as "The Next One." It might explain why the Hall took six years to induct him once Lindros became eligible in 2011. First, he snubbed Sault Ste. Marie in junior, then slighted Quebec, his NHL draft team, not because he didn't like "the people, the province, a city or the culture. It was owner (Marcel Aubut)," said Lindros. Further, he always seemed engulfed in management issues. When Lindros wouldn't sign, Aubut carelessly traded him to two teams before an arbitrator validated the Philadelphia deal, which cost general manager Bobby Clarke six players, two first-round picks and $15 million. But Lindros came as advertised and won the Hart Trophy in 1994–95 and scored a career-high 115 points the next season. There was one Stanley Cup appearance (a sweep by Detroit in 1997), followed by a lot of headaches for Clarke from the Lindros family. Then, beginning in March 1998, Lindros' status fell as arguably hockey's best player to its most unbankable after suffering six concussions in a 27-month period. Lindros came with a lot of baggage, but travels in good company among Hart's youngest MVPs.

Eric Lindros

The NHL's Youngest Hart Trophy Winners

Player	Induction Year	1st Hart Year	Scoring	Age
Wayne Gretzky	1999	1979–80	51-86-137	19.5
Sidney Crosby		2006–07	36-84-120	19.8
Bobby Orr	1979	1969–70	33-87-120	22.3
Eric Lindros	2016	1994–95	29-41-70	22.4
Mario Lemieux	1997	1987–88	70-98-168	22.7

184

100 False

While no team has drafted more Hall members than
Montreal, among general managers, Glen Sather's success
at the draft is unsurpassed. Between 1979 and 1981, he
turned the expansion Edmonton Oilers into a dynasty,
cherry-picking five future Hall of Famers—a major heist
considering the Oilers started as the last seed in 1979's
21-team draft. But Sather never managed the one-two
punch of Bill Torrey, who built the New York Islanders into
four-time champions by snapping up Clark Gillies and then
Bryan Trottier in 1974's top-two rounds. Gillies earned Hall
status in 2002 and Trottier in 1997.

Most Hall of Famers Drafted by an NHL Team

NHL Team	Players (Draft Year, Induction Year)	NHL Team	Players (Draft Year, Induction Year)
Montreal — 9 Hall of Famers	Guy Lafleur (1971, 1988)	Edmonton — 5 Hall of Famers	Jari Kurri (1980, 2001)
	Vladislav Tretiak (1983, 1989)		Grant Fuhr (1981, 2003)
	Bob Gainey (1973, 1992)		Paul Coffey (1980, 2004)
	Steve Shutt (1972, 1993)		Mark Messier (1979, 2007)
	Larry Robinson (1971, 1995)		Glenn Anderson (1979, 2008)
	Viacheslav Fetisov* (1978, 2001)	New York Islanders — 5 Hall of Famers	Denis Potvin (1973, 1991)
	Rod Langway (1977, 2002)		Mike Bossy (1977, 1991)
	Patrick Roy (1984, 2006)		Bryan Trottier (1974, 1997)
	Chris Chelios (1981, 2013)		Clark Gillies (1974, 2002)
*Fetisov reentered draft in 1983			Pat LaFontaine (1983, 2003)

Questions 101-104

Cammi Granato and Angela James

101 Even though Cammi Granato and Angela James were great players, they were elected as Builders in the Hall of Fame because of their roles in the advancement of women's hockey. True or false?

102 Every Hall of Fame goalie has his name on the Stanley Cup, except non-NHLer Vladislav Tretiak of the Soviet Union. True or false?

103 As of 2016, Mike Eruzione, captain of the USA's Miracle on Ice team who won the 1980 Olympic gold medal in hockey, is not a member of either the Hockey Hall of Fame or the United States Hockey Hall of Fame. True or false?

104 No one has ever resigned from the Hall of Fame. True or false?

Mike Eruzione

Geraldine Heaney

101 False

Since the Hall revised its selection procedures so that women could be judged on their own merits, Angela James, Cammi Granato, Geraldine Heaney and Angela Ruggiero have all been enshrined in the Player category. "I look at this as being a great day for female hockey," said James, a 2010 inductee. Heaney echoed James later in 2013: "It was a male game when I played as a kid. Going down to the Hall of Fame you'd never see any females in there. You really didn't think, 'Could this ever happen?' I'm so glad it has." Heaney played 18 seasons and won Olympic gold in 2002 and silver in 1998 and seven World Championships. Ruggiero, who competed in four Olympics for Team USA, was honored in 2015.

**Roy Worters, Chuck Rayner,
Eddie Giacomin and Emile Francis**

102 False

Playing on Broadway does wonders post-retirement—
especially for netminders without a Stanley Cup. Besides
Vladislav Tretiak, the Hall's selection committee has
recognized only four other Cup-less goalies, all with long
careers backstopping NHL-based teams in one city: New
York. Hall of Famers Roy Worters, Chuck Rayner, Emile
Francis and Eddie Giacomin played with either the Rangers
or the Americans, and none ever won a league championship. Cup-less inductee Oliver Seibert was recognized for
his netminding duties by the Hall, but he was primarily a
skater during his career.

The Cup-less Goalie Greats of New York

Player	Induction Year	Career	Team	GP	Record	GAA	SO
Roy Worters	1969	1925–1937	NY Americans	484	171-229-83	2.27	67
Chuck Rayner	1973	1940–1953	NY Rangers	424	138-208-77	3.05	25
Eddie Giacomin	1987	1965–1978	NY Rangers	609	289-209-96	2.82	54
Emile Francis*	1982	1946 –1952	NY Rangers	95	31-52-11	3.76	1

* Emile Francis was elected to the Builder's category. In his 95-game career he played
   22 matches with the Rangers.

Mike Eruzione

103 True

For little-known amateur Mike Eruzione, nothing would be the same after February 22, 1980. At the Olympic Center in Lake Placid, Eruzione led an unheralded squad of collegians against the mighty Soviets and accomplished the unimaginable by helping the Americans claw out a stunning 4–3 victory. Two days later, USA struck Olympic gold in an amazing three-goal third-period comeback versus Finland, but it was Eruzione's winning marker against the Soviets that captured a nation. The dramatic upset was so shocking it became known as the Miracle on Ice. Eruzione would never play in the NHL. To date, as a player inductee, he is not in any of the three major Halls of Fame, including the International Ice Hockey Federation Hall of Fame.

104 False

The first and only member to resign from the Hall of Fame is Alan Eagleson. Once the sport's most influential person, Eagleson grew the game as a super-agent, the founder of the NHL players' union and an organizer of international hockey. His fall from powerbroker to pariah came with his 1997 criminal prosecution on fraud and theft charges over pension fund misuse. The events rocked the hockey world to its core and led 18 Hall of Famers to threaten to quit the Hall if the board let Eagleson remain a member. The disgraced union chief resigned in March 1998, nine years after his induction.

Alan Eagleson

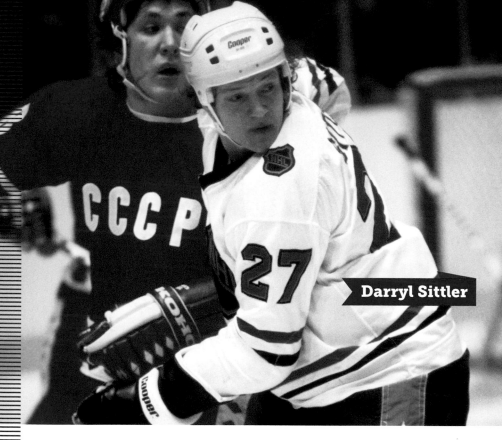

Darryl Sittler

105 Every NHLer named to the first-ever First and Second All-Star Teams of 1930–31 became a Hall of Fame member. True or false?

106 All of the five Canadian skaters on the ice when Darryl Sittler scored the climactic 1976 Canada Cup winner later became Hall members? True or false?

107 Although several Hall of Famers from hockey's early days, such as Bill Cook, Frank Boucher and Bun Cook (also known as the A Line), had careers in both the NHL and other pro leagues that competed for the Stanley Cup, no Hall members have won Cups on teams from more than one league. True or false?

108 A Hall member in the Builder category actually scored a Stanley Cup—winning goal. True or false?

The A Line: (L—R) Bill Cook, Frank Boucher and Bun Cook

Howie Morenz

105 True

The NHL's inaugural All-Star Team of 1930–31 boasted a legendary lineup of hockey pioneers. Each player and coach from that year eventually skated into the Hall, a promising start for the All-Star Team model. Only five other All-Star Teams featured an entire roster of future Hall of Famers, the last being 1960–61, which included the greatest names of the Original Six era.

The All-Star Teams of 1930–31

First All-Star Team					
Player	**Induction Year**	**Team**	**Position**	**GP**	**Scoring**
Charlie Gardiner	1945	Chicago	Goalie	44	24-17-3*
Eddie Shore	1947	Boston	Defense	44	15-16-31
King Clancy	1958	Toronto	Defense	44	7-14-21
Howie Morenz	1945	Montreal	Center	39	28-23-51
Bill Cook	1952	NY Rangers	Right wing	43	30-12-42
Aurèle Joliat	1947	Montreal	Left wing	43	13-22-35

Second All-Star Team					
Player	**Induction Year**	**Team**	**Position**	**GP**	**Scoring**
Tiny Thompson	1959	Boston	Goalie	44	28-10-6*
Sylvio Mantha	1960	Montreal	Defense	44	4-7-11
Ching Johnson	1958	NY Rangers	Defense	44	2-6-8
Frank Boucher	1958	NY Rangers	Center	44	12-27-39
Dit Clapper	1947	Boston	Right wing	43	22-8-30
Bun Cook	1995	NY Rangers	Left wing	44	18-17-35

* Netminding W-L-T stats

106 True

The 1976 Canada Cup was the first true international best-on-best hockey event. It featured the finest players from the top six nations, competing in a round-robin series followed by a best-of-three final. While Bobby Orr dominated both play and headlines, Darryl Sittler fired the historic Cup winner in Game 2 overtime against Czechoslovakia. Five future Hall of Famers played a part in the goal against Vladimir Dzurilla. "All five of us on the ice for Team Canada touched the puck on the way to Darryl's goal," Lanny McDonald recalled in an hhof.com interview. "The puck went from Larry Robinson to Denis Potvin, up the boards to me and I threw it straight up centre to Marcel Dionne, who one-touched it to Darryl [Sittler]. Darryl had a step on the defenseman, and at the top of the faceoff circle, faked a shot ... took one step sideways and rifled the puck into the open net," said McDonald, adding, "If there's another feeling like winning the Canada Cup, I'd sure like to find it!"

Darryl Sittler

107 False

Before the NHL took control of Lord Stanley's bowl in 1926–27, teams from several leagues competed for the Cup. Player movement between circuits meant some individuals became Cup champions from multiple leagues. Among those fortunate few is goalie savior Hap Holmes, whose brilliance helped Toronto's first champions, the Blueshirts of the NHA, capture the Cup in 1914. During his 17-year career, Holmes played in all five top pro leagues in existence between 1912 and 1928, yet he was no journeyman. Lured to the Pacific Coast Hockey Association, he outdueled defending Cup champion Georges Vezina and the Montreal Canadiens to lead the 1916–17 Seattle Metropolitans to the first Cup won by a U.S.-based club. On loan to the Toronto Arenas the next year, Holmes earned another Cup during the NHL's inaugural season. Then, in 1924–25, Holmes' versatility and "nerveless" cage work with the Western Canada Hockey League Victoria Cougars produced the last non-NHL Cup winner. Holmes is the only goalie in history to win the Cup with four franchises—and he hoisted it representing four leagues.

Hap Holmes

Hap Holmes: The Hall of Fame's 4 × 4 Man

Season	League	Stanley Cup Team	Distinction
1913–14	NHA	Toronto Blueshirts	First Cup by Toronto team
1916–17	PCHA	Seattle Metropolitans	First Cup by U.S. team
1917–18	NHL	Toronto Arenas	First Cup by NHL team
1924–25	WCHL	Victoria Cougars	Last Cup won by non-NHL team

108 True

Among the few NHL players enshrined as Builders in the Hall, none have the playing credentials of Carl Voss. In 1933, Voss was named the league's top rookie with Detroit. Five years later, as a member of the Black Hawks, he stole the puck from Maple Leafs winger George Parsons at the Toronto net and slipped it past Turk Broda, handing Chicago the lead and its second Stanley Cup. But Voss' most significant contributions came as an executive while serving as the NHL's first referee-in-chief. Over a 15-year period beginning in 1950, Voss did everything possible to improve the quality of his officials. He initiated scouting and training programs to raise standards throughout the league, evaluating his men in stripes based on their ability to call a fair game. While Voss achieved some regard while playing center for eight teams in eight NHL seasons, nothing surpassed his efforts when he took up the whistle. He became an honored Builder in 1974.

Carl Voss

109 Vladislav Tretiak was both the first Russian-trained and the first European-trained player to be inducted into the Hall of Fame. True or false?

110 No NHLer has ever won a player trophy during the same season he coached in the league. True or false?

Vladislav Tretiak

111 Tough guy Red Horner is the only NHL penalty leader to be elected to the Hall of Fame. True or false?

112 The individual usually credited as the "inventor" or "founding father" of hockey is not in the Hall of Fame. True or false?

Vladislav Tretiak

109 True

Vladislav Tretiak became a household name among North American hockey audiences during 1972's Summit Series between Canada and the Soviet Union. Most experts figured the Canadians would crush the USSR's national team. Expectations were high—never before had Canada assembled a bench of its best NHLers to compete internationally. But the Soviets' explosive attack game was a huge surprise. As was Tretiak, whom Canadian scouts had written off as their opponent's biggest liability. However, Tretiak kicked out almost everything, surrendering only 31 goals on the 267 shots fired his way. He turned into a world-class goalie, sporting a record 10 World Championship gold medals, three golds and one silver from the Olympics and one Canada Cup. Tretiak retired in 1984 and broke the Hall barrier for other European-trained players in 1989. Following his acceptance, some 15 Europeans have gained induction into what Tretiak considered the "highest honor" of his sports life.

110 False

Montreal's trade of Doug Harvey to New York in 1961 was more about adding toughness (in Rangers brute Lou Fontinato) to the Canadiens' lineup than about the decline of Harvey's defensive skills. As proof, the following season Fontinato led the NHL with 167 penalty minutes for the Habs, and Harvey, who served as the Blueshirts' player-coach, snagged his seventh Norris Trophy as the league's top rearguard and directed his club to its first playoff appearance in four years. Harvey is the only NHL bench boss to be awarded a playing trophy in the same season he coached.

Doug Harvey

Lou Fontinato

Answers 111-112

111 False

Pierre Pilote

Today's NHL penalty leaders aren't likely to get Hall of Fame recognition, at least not with the frequency of old-time box kings. They were sometimes the scoring superstars of their era because players had to be their own enforcers, a role that diminished when teams made bench room for the designated policeman. The last Hall-bound penalty boss was Chicago's Pierre Pilote, who registered a league-high 165 minutes in 1960–61 and was inducted in 1975. Fifteen penalty leaders—all from the NHL's first six decades—have become Hall members.

Top NHL Penalty Leaders in the Hall of Fame

Player	Induction Year	Season as PIM Leader	PIM
Ted Lindsay	1966	1958–59	184
Pierre Pilote	1975	1960–61	165
Eddie Shore	1947	1927–28	165
Fern Flaman	1990	1954–55	150
Red Horner*	1965	1932–33	144
Red Dutton*	1958	1928–29	139
Nels Stewart	1952	1926–27	133
Maurice Richard	1961	1952–53	112
Joe Hall*	1961	1917–18	100

*Player had multiple seasons as NHL penalty leader.

112 True

Hockey has long debated its defining origins. While several communities from Windsor, Nova Scotia, to Deline in the Northwest Territories claim to be the game's birthplace, hockey was neither "born, invented or created—it just happened," as hockey historian Bill Fitsell observed. Variations of play evolved wherever weather made natural open ice. In Canada, that would be almost everywhere. However, unraveling the who, how and why usually leads to James Creighton, the Halifax-born engineer who codified rules and moved the game from the near-chaos on frozen ponds to a regulated sport first staged in a covered arena on March 3, 1875. On a cold night before 40 curious onlookers under the soft glow of gas lanterns at Montreal's Victoria Rink, winter's unofficial sport was born. Without any real sense of the moment, except as demonstrated by the sportsmanship of the 18 participants, Creighton had pioneered the first hockey match. So little was made of his bold innovation that Creighton rested in an unmarked grave in Ottawa until October 2009, when he was honored with a ceremony attended by Canadian prime minister Stephen Harper and the Society for International Hockey Research. In the spirit of Creighton's modesty, a simple headstone and a plaque praising his achievements marks his final sanctuary. Today, Creighton's role in the evolution of hockey is monumental—an invaluable step forward in the modern game's rise to popularity.

James Creighton

Triple Gold

• •

How many Hall of Famers can claim membership in the Triple Gold Club? Fewer than 30 players have won the three most important hockey titles: an Olympic tournament, the World Championship and the Stanley Cup. Among them, only a handful have become Hall members, and a few more are potential candidates to hockey's shrine. In this game, fill in the blanks with the years each Hall member or future Hall contender first achieved honors on the game's greatest stages.

For solutions, turn the page.

Peter Forsberg

Olympics
1984, 1994, 1998, 2002, 2006

World Championships
1978, 1982, 1991, 1992, 1994, 1997, 2004, 2005

Stanley Cups
1991, 1995, 1996, 1997, 2007

	Olympics	World Championships	Stanley Cups
Joe Sakic			
Viacheslav Fetisov			
Igor Larionov			
Brendan Shanahan			
Nicklas Lidstrom			
Scott Niedermayer			
Chris Pronger			
Peter Forsberg			
Jaromir Jagr			

Triple Gold
Solutions

	Olympics	World Championships	Stanley Cups
Joe Sakic	2002	1994	1996
Viacheslav Fetisov	1984	1978	1997
Igor Larionov	1984	1982	1997
Brendan Shanahan	2002	1994	1997

	Olympics	World Championships	Stanley Cups
Nicklas Lidstrom	2006	1991	1997
Scott Niedermayer	2002	2004	1995
Chris Pronger	2002	1997	2007
Peter Forsberg	1994	1992	1996
Jaromir Jagr	1998	2005	1991

Jaromir Jagr

Glenn Hall

Crease Magnets

The least-represented position in the Hall of Fame is the goalie. That may be because only two netminders are named to a 23-man roster, so fewer goalies than skaters are available for induction. Or it could be the demanding job qualifications. Stopping pucks is a complex art executed in real time under extreme pressure that requires, as *Time Magazine* described it, "the glove of an all-star shortstop, the agility of a gold-medal gymnast, the reflexes of a championship racing-car driver, the eye of a .400 hitter and the mind of a geometrician." Even then, mastering those fundamental skills is useless if the player doesn't have the DNA to conquer his fear factor associated with being the game's puck magnet.

113 Who was named to the NHL's First All-Star Team from all three clubs he backstopped?

A.
Terry Sawchuk

B.
Glenn Hall

C.
Patrick Roy

D.
Ed Belfour

114 Which goalie worked the most NHL games without winning a Stanley Cup during his Hall of Fame career?

A.
Chuck Rayner

B.
Harry Lumley

C.
Eddie Giacomin

D.
Bill Durnan

115 Which NHL first did Ken Dryden achieve as a NHL rookie?

A. He was named playoff MVP before winning top rookie honors

B. He was the first goalie to jump directly from junior to the NHL

C. He was the first goalie to face more than 2,000 shots in a season

D. All of the above

116 How many Hall of Fame goalies never played an NHL game?

A. Soviet star Vladislav Tretiak is the Hall's only non-NHL goalie

B. Two goalies

C. Five goalies

D. Eight goalies

Ken Dryden

113 B. Glenn Hall

Glenn Hall may be best known for owning the most unbeatable record in sports, with 502 consecutive starts in goal and, as it happened, throwing up prior to every one of them. However, his longevity at the highest level is distinguished by another remarkable feat. Hall is likely the only player in any professional team sport to collect a First All-Star Team berth on three different major-league clubs. On seven occasions he was voted a First All-Star, originally with Detroit in 1957, then with Chicago multiple times between 1958 and 1966 and lastly with St. Louis, his record third team, in 1969. Hall, who once said, "Playing goal is a winter of torture for me," was a league leader or award winner in a remarkable 13 of 14 seasons. His dominance in hockey won him every distinction available to a netminder, except the skater-favored Hart Trophy. He was honored by the Hall in 1975.

Glenn Hall's Hardware Haul

NHL Leader/Honors	Seasons
Games played	Led league eight seasons: 1955–56 to 1961–62 (70)*, 1965–66 (64)*
Wins	Led league four seasons: 1956–57 (38), 1962–63 (30), 1963–64 (34), 1965–66 (34)
Goals-against average	Led league one season: 1966–67 (2.38)
Shutouts	Led league six seasons: 1955–56 (12), 1959–60 (6), 1960–61 (6), 1961–62 (9), 1962–63 (5),* 1968–69 (8)
Vezina Trophy	Won award three seasons: 1963, 1967,* 1969*
1st All-Star berths	Named seven seasons: 1956–57, 1957–58, 1959–60, 1962–63, 1963–64, 1965–66, 1968–69
2nd All-Star berths	Named four seasons: 1955–56, 1960–61, 1961–62, 1966–67
Calder Trophy	Won top rookie award: 1956
Conn Smythe Trophy	Won playoff MVP award: 1968
Stanley Cup	Won NHL championship: 1961

*Shared honor

114 C. Eddie Giacomin

There are about 30 full-time netminders in the Hall of Fame, and just a few are without a Stanley Cup on their résumé. For the Cup-less Eddie Giacomin, his steady play with the New York Rangers during the 1960s and 1970s helped etch his name on a Hall plaque. He was a fan favorite, and his acrobatic saves won him everlasting affection at Madison Square Garden—even after he was claimed on waivers by Detroit late in his career. Only days after the transaction, Giacomin returned to MSG in an emotional homecoming seldom given a player in an opponent's uniform. Giacomin, toiling for the Red Wings, received numerous standing ovations throughout the game. Each save against the Rangers was met with the crowd's roar of "Edd-ie, Edd-ie." One former teammate even apologized for scoring in Giacomin's 6–4 victory by the Wings. Fast Eddie never made it to the top while playing for the Blueshirts, but he came within two wins of Lord Stanley's mug, only to bow to Boston in the 1972 final. The last NHL goalie inducted without a Cup win, Giacomin entered the Hall in 1987. Among his Hall peers, no one has more starts without being crowned a champion, 609 games.

Ken Dryden

115 A. He was named playoff MVP before winning top rookie honors

Three words describe Ken Dryden's remarkable NHL debut: Hall of Fame. His storybook start began with a late-season call up by Montreal in 1970–71. After just six regular-season games and a perfect 6-0-0, Dryden ambushed Bobby Orr's heavily favored Boston Bruins in the quarterfinal then knocked off the stubborn Minnesota North Stars. Finally, in a seven-game Stanley Cup thriller against Chicago, he outdueled Tony Esposito to hand the Canadiens their 17th Cup. In that spring of hockey heroics, the 23-year-old rookie kept Montreal in contention despite falling behind in two series and being peppered with 709 shots, an average of 34.8 shots per game. In just a matter of weeks, Dryden had established himself as the future of goaltending in Montreal. He won the Conn Smythe Trophy as playoff MVP, and the next season he registered a league-leading 39 wins to capture the Calder Trophy as top freshman, the first and only time an NHLer nabbed a Conn Smythe before his Calder prize.

116 C. Five goalies

Vladislav Tretiak is the only modern goalie without NHL experience in the Hall to date, but four other netminders were inducted for careers that pre-date the league. Each member of the quartet won multiple Stanley Cups with defunct clubs in hockey's formative years, when goalies wore little protection, had no defined goal creases and were required to remain standing at all times. Paddy Moran captured successive Cups with the Quebec Bulldogs and Percy LeSueur led the old Ottawa Senators to numerous titles. Riley Hern, one of the first professional goalies to backstop a Cup victor, championed the Montreal Wanderers, while Bouse Hutton backstopped the legendary Ottawa Silver Seven. Moran was minted by the Hall in 1958, LeSueur in 1961 and Hern and Hutton in 1962.

Hall of Fame Goalies Without NHL Experience

Player	Induction Year	Career	Most Prominent Leagues	Most Prominent Teams	Cups
Paddy Moran	1958	1905–1917	ECAHA NHA	Quebec Quebec	1912 1913
Percy LeSueur	1961	1906–1916	ECAHA NHA	Ottawa Ottawa, Toronto	1909 1910* 1911
Riley Hern	1962	1903–1911	IHL ECAHA NHA	Portage Lakes Montreal Wanderers Montreal Wanderers	1907 1908 1910*
Bouse Hutton	1962	1898–1909	CAHL	Ottawa	1903 1904
Vladislav Tretiak	1989	1968–1984	USSR International	CSKA Moscow Soviet National Team	

* When the Stanley Cup was a challenge trophy it was sometimes awarded more than once in a season. In 1910 it was won in January by Ottawa and in March by Montreal.

 Who came up with the idea of painting stitch marks on the celebrated mask of Hall of Fame goalie Gerry Cheevers?

A. An equipment manager

B. A young fan in a Bruins contest promotion

C. A catcher with the Boston Red Sox

D. Cheevers himself

118 How many netminders are immortalized with an NHL trophy named in their honor?

A. Only one, Georges Vezina

B. Two netminders

C. Three netminders

D. Four netminders

119

What nickname did old-timer Frank Brimsek earn after posting six shutouts in his first eight games as an NHL rookie?

A. Zilchy

B. The Eggman

C. Blank-em Frank

D. Mr. Zero

120

Which Hall of Famer is the oldest starting goalie ever to play in the NHL?

A.
Johnny Bower of the Toronto Maple Leafs

B.
Glenn Hall of the St. Louis Blues

C.
Gump Worsley of the Minnesota North Stars

D.
Jacques Plante of the Toronto Maple Leafs

117 D. Cheevers himself

The stitchwork motif of Gerry Cheevers' famed mask was his own inspiration. The Bruins puckstopper had been trying to duck practice after passing out from a shot to his noggin, but coach Harry Sinden coaxed him back on the ice. According to Cheevers, "I turned to Frosty Forristall, our trainer, and said, 'Frosty, paint a stitch mark or two on the mask,' so he painted this big gouge over the right eye and it got a laugh. We started to paint stitches every time I got hit. Frosty would calculate where it would have been and how many stitches it would have taken." Although Cheevers never claimed an individual award, the best goals-against average or an All-Star berth, his playoff record made him a big-time goalie and paved his way to the Hall of Fame. He won 53 of 88 playoff matches and two Stanley Cups in Boston. Cheevers was inducted in 1985, five years after his retirement.

118 A. Only one, Georges Vezina

Several peers were considered his equal, but no other guardian from hockey's early days is more famous than Georges Vezina, the stalwart netminder of the Montreal Canadiens whose legacy is perpetuated by the Vezina Trophy. Remarkably, Vezina never missed a match in 15 years of play, with a streak of 367 consecutive starts before his collapse in the Canadiens' first contest of 1925–26. His sudden death from tuberculosis months later prompted the club to donate the Vezina Trophy to honor his memory. Vezina was among the original 11 individuals elected to the Hall of Fame in 1945. Today, the Vezina goes to the best netminder as voted by NHL general managers.

Turk Broda with Vezina Trophy

Frank Brimsek

119 D. Mr. Zero

Among all the accolades awarded to Frank Brimsek in his rookie season, including the 1939 Stanley Cup, the best-remembered tribute may be the nickname bestowed upon him by adoring Boston fans. Brought in to replace 10-year Bruins veteran Tiny Thompson—whose trade to Detroit was likened to the disastrous Red Sox swap of Babe Ruth— Brimsek had big skates to fill. After losing his first game, the rookie posted three straight zeroes, breaking Thompson's club record with a sparkling 231 minutes and 54 seconds of shutout hockey. Not done, Brimsek banged out three more zilches for six in his first eight games—all in December 1939. By season's end, Bruins fans were asking "Tiny who?" Brimsek's 10 goose eggs in his freshman year had won their hearts and won him everlasting fame as Mr. Zero.

Frank Brimsek's Baptism by Fire

Games 1–8, December 1938							
Date	Rival	GA	Score	Date	Rival	GA	Score
Dec. 1	Montreal	2	2–0 L	Dec. 13	Montreal	2	3–2 W
Dec. 4	Chicago	0	5–0 W	Dec. 15	Montreal	0	1–0 W
Dec. 6	Chicago	0	2–0 W	Dec. 18	Detroit	0	2–0 W
Dec. 11	NY Rangers	0	3–0 W	Dec. 20	NY Americans	0	3–0 W

Other Honors: Calder; Vezina; regular season leader in GAA (1.56), wins (33) and shutouts (10); playoff leader in wins (8); 1st All-Star; played in 1939 All-Star Game; 1939 Stanley Cup

120 A. Johnny Bower of the Toronto Maple Leafs

They called Johnny Bower the China Wall because he was an ageless wonder who stopped practically everything. Between his AHL and NHL action, Bower worked more games than any other netminder, enduring 12 years in the minors before starting full time with Toronto in 1958–59— at 34 years old. By comparison, late-bloomer Tim Thomas was 31 when he became the Bruins number-one man in 2005–06. Bower proved to be hockey's great warhorse. He braved 25 seasons of pain and punishment, battling the game ill-equipped and under-coached, always facing the fear of serious injury, employment uncertainty and public scrutiny. He survived intact, winning four Stanley Cups and becoming the oldest netminder to appear in a playoff game at 44 years old. He strapped on his worn pads a final time at age 45 in December 1969.

121 Who entered the Hall of Fame with the most career penalty minutes?

A.
Hap Holmes

B.
Billy Smith

C.
Gerry Cheevers

D.
Bernie Parent

122 Who was the fastest to 100 NHL wins?

A.
Harry Lumley of the
Detroit Red Wings

B.
Bill Durnan of the
Montreal Canadiens

C.
Terry Sawchuk of the
Detroit Red Wings

D.
Grant Fuhr of the
Edmonton Oilers

123

Old-time goalie Percy LeSueur's multi-faceted hockey career earned him a Hall of Fame reputation as:

A.
A man who was ahead of his time

B.
A goalie with the IQ of Einstein

C.
A goalie with the puckhandling skills of a superstar center

D.
A man who could have been prime minister of Canada

124

Which puckstopper was responsible for forcing the NHL to adopt a rule banning goalies from freezing a puck outside the crease?

A.
Charlie Gardiner of the
Chicago Black Hawks

B.
Eddie Giacomin of the
New York Rangers

C.
Jacques Plante of the
Montreal Canadiens

D.
Tony Esposito of the
Chicago Black Hawks

121 B. Billy Smith

Billy Smith earned his reputation for hard-edged competitiveness almost immediately. In his NHL rookie season of 1972–73, he dropped the gloves with Rangers winger Rod Gilbert to receive the first fighting major assessed to the expansion New York Islanders. In 37 games that season he was assessed 42 minutes, a league record for goalies. It was a jaw-dropping start for Battlin' Billy or, as he later became known, Hatchet Man. To give himself "working room" around the net, he hacked and whacked encroaching forwards with a vengeance—once reportedly breaking three sticks in one game on the ankles of Buffalo players. Later, after Smith butt-ended Lindy Ruff in the eye in 1980, the NHL required all goalies to have a large knob at the end of their stick's handle. The league also enlarged the goal crease to a 6-foot semicircle, thanks in part to Smith's predatory tactics. By his retirement, Smith had amassed 489 regular-season penalty minutes and another 89 during the postseason. He never registered great goals-against averages but delivered in the playoffs, with 88 victories in 132 appearances, and brought four straight Stanley Cups to the Isles. His induction came four years after he wielded his last Koho paddle in 1989.

122 B. Bill Durnan of the Montreal Canadiens

Bill Durnan garnered the kind of career success that's nearly impossible to achieve, given his brief time in the NHL spotlight. In seven short years during the 1940s, Durnan won the Vezina Trophy six times, a number equal to his illustrious string of First All-Star Team appearances. In his rookie campaign, he guided the Canadiens to a 22-0-3 record at the Forum to net the NHL's longest home-undefeated streak from a season start. The stretch helped Durnan to a little-known mark for the fastest 100 wins to begin a career. He did it in 139 games and on a very good team that played against lineups stocked with several wartime replacements—a handicap that never severely affected Montreal. His sterling career included two Stanley Cups and a modern-day record for the league's longest shutout sequence, eclipsed only in 2003–04 by Brian Boucher of Phoenix. But stress and a legion of injuries finally got Durnan. He abruptly quit hockey after three straight losses to the New York Rangers during the 1950 semifinal, a goalie broken but unbowed.

Bill Durnan: The NHL's Fastest 100-Win Goalie

Season	GP	Record	GAA	Career Wins to Date
1943–44	50	38-5-7	2.18	38 wins in 50 games
1944–45	50	38-8-4	2.42	76 wins in 100 games
1945–46	40	24-11-5	2.60	100 wins in 139 games

Milestone win came in second-last match of 1945–46, Durnan's 139th career game, a 6–3 victory vs. Chicago on March 16. His record was 100-23-16.

123 A. A man who was ahead of his time

While several goalies are credited with making innovative changes to game play and equipment, Percy LeSueur might just be the brightest and most important netminder among hockey's trendsetters. LeSueur's early fame came while he was backstopping the Ottawa Senators to three Stanley Cups before the NHL began in 1917. However, he was equally successful in the technical aspects of the sport. During his playing career, he wrote *How to Play Hockey*, a 48-page handbook that detailed game intricacies for all positions on the ice. Two years later, the NHA adopted his designs for the first goal net that could trap rising shots. LeSueur became a coach, manager, referee, arena manager, radio commentator and columnist, but he was first a student of the game. Always "ahead of his time," as noted by Hall of Fame broadcaster Budd Lynch, LeSueur also devised a gauntlet-type glove to protect a goalie's forearm, introduced the idea of afternoon games to attract spectators and started "shots on goal" statistics in box scores. Peerless Percy graduated to the Hall in 1961.

Percy LeSueur

124 C. Jacques Plante of the Montreal Canadiens

Jacques Plante was affectionately nicknamed Jake the Snake for his lightning-quick forays around the net, but when he ventured outside his crease to smother a loose puck for a stoppage in play, opposing coaches and fans weren't so complimentary. They complained it slowed the game. In fact, the Canadiens netminder froze the puck so adeptly, the NHL created Rule 63.2—or the Plante rule—in 1959, which stated that a goaltender could only fall on or cover the puck inside the crease. Undeterred, Plante continued to roam behind the net. He became the first goalie to stop opponent shoot-ins, enabling his team to quickly counterattack. And he was the first to raise his arm to signal an icing call for his defensemen. "Possession of the puck is No. 1," Plante said, adding, "That's all I'm doing, getting control until one of my teammates comes along."

Questions 125-128

125 Which Hall of Famer registered the most career wins by an undrafted NHL netminder?

A.
Ken Dryden

B.
Hap Holmes

C.
Bernie Parent

D.
Ed Belfour

126 Despite owning the NHL record for most consecutive wins in more than one playoff year, which goalie has not been elected to the Hall of Fame?

A.
Mike Richter
of the New York
Rangers

B.
Andy Moog
of the Edmonton
Oilers

C.
Curtis Joseph
of the Toronto
Maple Leafs

D.
Tom Barrasso
of the Pittsburgh
Penguins

127 Who is the last maskless tandem to win the Stanley Cup?

A.
Johnny Bower and Terry Sawchuk
of the Toronto Maple Leafs

B.
Gump Worsley and Rogie Vachon
of the Montreal Canadiens

C.
Gerry Cheevers and Eddie Johnston
of the Boston Bruins

D.
Bernie Parent and Wayne
Stephenson of the Philadelphia
Flyers

128 Which Hall of Fame goalie led the NHL in goals-against average on a non-playoff team?

A.
Roy Worters of
the New York
Americans

B.
Alex Connell
of the Ottawa
Senators

C.
Paddy Moran
of the Quebec
Bulldogs

D.
Chuck Rayner
of the New York
Rangers

125 D. Ed Belfour

Ed Belfour made a habit of defying his critics. When the scouts said he wasn't NHL material and left him undrafted out of the University of North Dakota in 1987, Belfour signed with Chicago and led the league in games, wins, minutes and goals-against to claim the 1991 Calder Trophy as top rookie. When they said he couldn't win big games, Belfour hoisted a Stanley Cup with Dallas in 1999. At his retirement in 2007, the underrated stopper nobody wanted had amassed 484 wins in 18 years, the most victories and the longest career by a former free agent. Not bad for a guy who had slipped under everyone's radar. He silenced his critics for good with his Hall enshrinement in 2011.

Ed Belfour: Hockey's Hidden Gem

NHL Career Stats (1988–2007)								
Regular Season								
Teams	GP	Record	GA	SA	SV	SV%	GAA	SO
Chicago, San Jose, Dallas, Toronto, Florida	963	484-320-125	2317	24751	22434	.906	2.50	76
Playoffs								
Teams	GP	Record	GA	SA	SV	SV%	GAA	SO
Chicago, Dallas, Toronto	161	88-68	359	4476	4117	.920	2.17	14

126 D. Tom Barrasso of the Pittsburgh Penguins

By the time he retired in 2003, Tom Barrasso had become one of the greatest American goalies in NHL play. He had won it all, except the hearts and minds of the media. Known for his arrogance, at least during some of his career, Barrasso joined Buffalo at 18 years old, a student of Massachusetts' Acton-Boxborough High School. Without playing one game on the farm, he captured the Vezina Trophy with a 2.84 goals-against average, won the Calder Trophy as top rookie and was elected to the First All-Star Team, all in 1983–84. Later, with Pittsburgh, his contributions played a major role in the 1991 and 1992 Stanley Cups, and he netted a league-record 14 straight wins during in 1992's and 1993's playoffs. Barrasso also shares the NHL mark for most consecutive wins in one playoff year (11) with Ed Belfour and Patrick Roy, who are both in the Hall of Fame.

Tom Barrasso's Brilliant Victory Run

The NHL's Longest Playoff Winning Streak by a Goalie		
Season	Wins	Record Wins
1992*	11	3 wins vs. NY Rangers in DF, 4 wins vs. Boston in CF, 4 wins vs. Chicago in F, won Stanley Cup
1993	3	3 wins vs. New Jersey in DSF, lost DF
Total	14	

*Single-playoff-year record

Gump Worsley

Rogie Vachon

127 B. Gump Worsley and Rogie Vachon of the Montreal Canadiens

Few Stanley Cup tandems have ever become Hall of Famers. Johnny Bower and Terry Sawchuk did, and with Rogie Vachon's induction in 2016, he and Gump Worsley succeeded, not only in this Hall rarity as a Cup-winning duo but as the last barefaced champions. Ironically, the Canadiens are the same team to ice both the first masked goalie and the last maskless goalies to win Cups, Jacques Plante in 1960 and nine years later Worsley and Vachon. During their three-round Cup drive of 1969, Worsley started, boasting a 15-playoff game unbeaten streak. But knee problems and a puffy hand forced him out of the net, which brought Vachon between the pipes. They split the most important series, a second round, six-game duel against Boston, three apiece, with Vachon capturing Game 6's 2-1 series clincher in the second overtime period. The Cup itself was on the line, considering their final opponent would be the expansion St. Louis Blues. It might have been Vachon's greatest performance of his 843-game career. He stoned the Bruins, stopping 50 of 51 shots, including 22 in the second frame. As predicted, the Canadiens, backed by Vachon in the final, easily swept St. Louis for the Cup. All successive Cup victors, including Gerry Cheevers, Ken Dryden and Bernie Parent, wore face protection.

128 A. Roy Worters of the New York Americans

Had Roy "Shrimp" Worters not measured 5-foot-3, a more apt nickname might have been "Rubber Magnet," in recognition of all the pucks he attracted in his 12-year career. During the 1920s and 1930s, Worters plied his trade with two of hockey's most frequent cellar-dwellers, the Pittsburgh Pirates and the New York Americans, yet he still amassed a remarkable 67 shutouts. In 1930–31, while goal-scoring was on the rise, Worters, who stood barely a foot above the crossbar, notched eight zeroes in the NHL's 44-game schedule and won the Vezina Trophy, icing a league-best 1.61 goals-against average on 74 goals allowed. Despite those numbers, the anemic Americans couldn't make the playoffs, mustering only 76 goals to finish seventh in the 10-team NHL circuit. Worters is the only NHL starter to lead the league in goals-against with a non-playoff team. Elected in 1969, Shrimp is the Hall's shortest player.

Roy Worters' Season of Futility

1930–31 NHL Standings							
Team	GP	Record	GF	GA	Pts.	Goalie	GAA
Boston	44	28-10-6	143	90	62	Tiny Thompson	1.98
Montreal	44	26-10-8	129	89	60	George Hainsworth	1.95
Toronto	44	22-13-9	118	99	53	Lorne Chabot*	2.09
Chicago	44	24-17-3	108	78	51	Charlie Gardiner	1.73
NY Rangers	44	19-16-9	106	87	47	John Roach	1.89
Mtl. Maroons	44	20-18-6	105	106	46	Dave Kerr*	2.37
NY Americans	44	18-16-10	76	74	46	Roy Worters	1.61
Detroit	44	16-21-7	102	105	39	Dolly Dolson	2.29
Ottawa	44	10-30-4	91	142	24	Alex Connell*	3.01
Philadelphia	44	4-36-4	76	184	12	Wilf Cude*	4.22

*Shared season, played most games for team

129 Who is the first NHL netminder to receive credit for an assist on an intentional pass that led to a goal?

A.
Tiny Thompson of the Boston Bruins

B.
Clint Benedict of the Montreal Maroons

C.
Georges Vezina of the Montreal Canadiens

D.
It isn't known who recorded the first assist by a goalie

130 Which goalie backstopped his team to an NHL playoff record of 10 over-time wins?

A.
Terry Sawchuk of the Detroit Red Wings

B.
Terry Sawchuk of the Toronto Maple Leafs

C.
Patrick Roy of the Montreal Canadiens

D.
Patrick Roy of the Colorado Avalanche

131 Old-timer Clint Benedict is recognized today for which NHL first?

A.
He was the first goalie to wear a mask

B.
He was the first goalie to cause a rule change

C.
He was the first goalie on two different Stanley Cup champion teams

D.
All of the above

132 Who was named top rookie in three different leagues before achieving NHL stardom?

A.
Glenn Hall of Humboldt, Saskatchewan

B.
Terry Sawchuk of Winnipeg, Manitoba

C.
Grant Fuhr of Spruce Grove, Alberta

D.
Ed Belfour of Carman, Manitoba

129 A. Tiny Thompson of the Boston Bruins

Until Boston great Tiny Thompson was credited with an assist on a Babe Siebert breakaway goal against Toronto in January 1936, netminders had attracted little attention in scoring statistics. After the game, hockey experts believed his calculated play for the assist had set a precedent. In fairness, goaltenders had assisted on goals before Thompson, but they had likely never earned the point in the game summaries. Interestingly, a *Globe and Mail* game account had the official scorer giving Thompson "assists on both goals by Siebert" in the 4−1 Bruins win. Today, the NHL only credits Thompson with one assist in the match.

130 C. Patrick Roy of the Montreal Canadiens

No team has ever duplicated Montreal's astonishing run of overtime victories during the 1993 Stanley Cup playoffs. The postseason belonged to Patrick Roy. Backstopping a near-pedestrian lineup of Canadiens, Roy played the best clutch hockey in history, giving his teammates the time to score game winners in 10 overtimes through 20 playoff matches (the next best is seven OT wins). Player for player, the Canadiens were "in the zone" behind Roy, chuckling in the dressing room about who would deliver the next OT winner. Montreal set an NHL record for most one-goal wins in a post-season (12), and Roy was presented the Conn Smythe Trophy, his second of three playoff MVP prizes.

Patrick Roy's Hall of Fame 1993 Overtime Streak

Game	Date	GA	SA	SV	SV%	Ice Time	Score
DSF vs. Quebec Nordiques (4–2)							
1	Apr. 22	1	35	34	.971	70:30	2–1 OT W
2	Apr. 26	2	37	35	.946	50:03	5–4 OT W*
DF vs. Buffalo Sabres (4–0)							
3	May 4	3	31	28	.903	62:50	4–3 OT W
4	May 6	3	36	33	.917	68:28	4–3 OT W
5	May 8	3	40	37	.925	71:37	4–3 OT W
CF vs. New York Islanders (4–1)							
6	May 18	3	42	39	.929	86:21	4–3 2OT W
7	May 20	1	32	31	.969	72:34	2–1 OT W
F vs. Los Angeles Kings (4–1)							
8	Jun. 3	2	24	22	.917	60:19	3–2 OT W
9	Jun. 5	3	30	30	.909	60:34	4–3 OT W
10	Jun. 7	2	40	40	.952	74.37	3–2 OT W

*Shared win with André Racicot (ice time: 18:14)

Clint Benedict

131 D. All of the above

Clint Benedict was a game-changer in sport's truest sense. When the NHL restricted goalies to a standing-only position in hockey's early days, Benedict became an expert at accidentally losing his balance and falling to the ice to smother the puck. Other net guardians copied Benedict's deceptive tactics, and the league changed the rule in January 1918, allowing stoppers to drop to the ice to make saves. After Ottawa sold his services to the Montreal Maroons in 1924, he guided them to the Stanley Cup, becoming the first NHL goalie to backstop two different Cup winners, the Senators in 1921 and 1923 and the Maroons in 1926. And when Benedict's nose and cheekbone were smashed by a Howie Morenz shot in 1930, he briefly wore a crude leather mask, a league first that came 29 years before Jacques Plante changed the look of goaltenders forever. Benedict took his place among hockey's elite in 1965.

132 B. Terry Sawchuk of Winnipeg, Manitoba

Few general managers have ever traded away a Stanley Cup–winning goalie for a rookie netminder, but when Detroit's Jack Adams saw Terry Sawchuk perform between the pipes, he knew he was looking at crease perfection. Adams was so impressed with Sawchuk after just seven NHL games that he dumped Cup veteran Harry Lumley and made the 20-year-old newbie from Winnipeg his starter. Adams' gamble paid off immediately. After being crowned top rookie with Omaha in the United States Hockey League in 1947–48 then repeating the honor with Indianapolis the next year in the American Hockey League, Sawchuk led the NHL in wins and shutouts to capture the Calder Trophy in 1950–51. Sawchuk had netted a triple crown of freshman awards in a four-year span. His 44 victories as an NHL rookie are unequaled in league action, although fellow Hall of Famer Ed Belfour registered 43 with Chicago in 1990–91.

Terry Sawchuk: Rookie of the Century

Season	Team	League	GP	Record	GA	SO	Avg.
1947–48	Omaha Knights	USHL	54	30-18-5	174	4*	3.21
1948–49	Indianapolis Capitols	AHL	67	38-17-2	205	2	3.06
1950–51	Detroit Red Wings	NHL	70*	44*-13-13	139	11*	1.99

*League leader

The Twilight Zone

• •

Hall of Famer Stan Mikita produced the highest penalty count by an Art Ross Trophy winner as well as the lowest box-time total ever registered in 70 or more games. Within two seasons of collecting his record-high 154 minutes, Mikita went from sinner to saint and dropped to just 12 minutes during his 97-point title in 1966–67. Welcome to the twilight zone of hockey statistics: the offbeat, rare achievements that break all the rules. In this game, match the Hall member with his unofficial NHL record.

For solutions, turn the page.

Part 1

Player	Record	Player	Record
Mario Lemieux	168	Harry Lumley	17
Brett Hull	86	Frank Nighbor	40
Peter Forsberg	166	Doug Gilmour	35
Steve Yzerman	155		

1.	Most penalty minutes by a Lady Byng Trophy winner
2.	Fewest shots on goal by an NHL scoring champion (minimum 70 games)
3.	Most points by a player not voted an NHL All-Star
4.	Age of the youngest NHL goalie
5.	Most goals without winning the NHL scoring title
6.	Most points by a player on a non-playoff team
7.	Most playoff points by a player whose team did not reach the Stanley Cup Final

Part 2

Player	Record	Player	Record
Jari Kurri	71	Red Kelly	18
Mike Gartner	708	Adam Oates	114
Luc Robitaille	171	Wayne Gretzky	-25
Gordie Howe	40		

1.	Worst plus-minus by a scoring champion
2.	Fewest penalty minutes by a Norris Trophy winner
3.	Most career goals by a player never voted an NHL All-Star
4.	Lowest draft pick to score 500 goals
5.	Most playoff assists by a player who never won the Stanley Cup
6.	Most goals without winning the NHL goal-scoring title
7.	Age of the oldest player to record his first 100th regular-season point

Peter Forsberg

The Twilight Zone

Solutions

Part 1

1. The first two Lady Byng winners, **Frank Nighbor** and Billy Burch, set the bar for penalty minutes at 40. No winner of the NHL's best sportsman trophy has topped their penalty total since 1926–27.

2. **Peter Forsberg** and Henrik Sedin led the NHL with 106 points in 2002–03 and 112 points in 2009–10. Each scored 29 goals on 166 shots, the lowest in NHL history by a scoring champion.

3. It was **Steve Yzerman**'s career year of 155 points, good enough for third overall in 1988–89's scoring race, but behind First and Second All-Star centers Mario Lemieux (199 points) and Wayne Gretzky (168 points).

4. The war years sapped the NHL of great players, who were often replaced by fresh faces, none younger in nets than future Hall of Famer **Harry Lumley**, who at 17 played a two-game tryout with Detroit in 1943–44.

5. **Brett Hull** more than doubled Wayne Gretzky's 41-goal count with 86 goals, but Gretzky tripled Hull in assists, 122 to 45, which gave No. 99 another scoring title: 163 points to Hull's 131 in 1990–91.

6. **Mario Lemieux**'s first scoring title is one of hockey's great unofficial records in futility: in 1987–88 he scored 168 points as Pittsburgh sank to last place with 81 points in the Patrick Division.

7. Toronto missed the 1993 Stanley Cup final by one goal after losing to Los Angeles 5–4 in Game 7 of the conference finals, as **Doug Gilmour** scored 35 points (second only to Wayne Gretzky), the most ever by a player who didn't reach the Cup Final.

Part 2

1. Nine years after recording the NHL's best plus-minus of plus-98 by a scoring leader, **Wayne Gretzky** posted a minus-25 in his league-leading 130-point season of 1993–94, the worst plus-minus by a title holder.

2. **Red Kelly** and Nicklas Lidstrom took defense to a new level of clean play, with a Norris Trophy–low of just 18 minutes, Kelly in 1953–54 and Lidstrom in 2000–01.

3. In his 19-year career **Mike Gartner** was never voted an NHL All-Star. However, he did finish in sixth place overall among goal-scoring leaders with 708 goals, the most career markers by a non-All-Star.

4. Lucky **Luc Robitaille** waited until Los Angeles selected him 171st overall in 1984. He would score 668 goals, the most by any left winger in NHL history.

5. **Adam Oates** set up more postseason goals than any other NHLer without a Stanley Cup: 114 assists.

6. A 71-goal season should lock up the NHL's goal-scoring crown, but **Jari Kurri** finished two goals short of Edmonton linemate Wayne Gretzky, who potted 73 goals in 1984–85.

7. One day shy of his 41st birthday, **Gordie Howe** scored his 100th point of 1968–69, a career first that came in his 23rd NHL season.

Al MacInnis

Blood, Sweat and Cheers

The Hall of Fame's 2007 quartet of NHL players may be its greatest class. No group of inductees has combined to score more than Mark Messier, Al MacInnis, Scott Stevens and Ron Francis, who collectively compiled 5,867 career points in 6,538 games—both numbers are Hall records for a class of honorees. All four men were recognized in their first year of eligibility, after playing their last games in 2003–04. In this chapter, we celebrate the Hall's own record-makers.

133 What is the shortest span of time between a player's final NHL game and his Hall induction?

A. The same day

B. Within a month of retirement

C. Within six months of retirement

D. Within one year of retirement

134 Which Hall of Famer amassed the highest regular-season penalty-minute total?

A.
Brendan Shanahan of the
St. Louis Blues

B.
Paul Coffey of the
Pittsburgh Penguins

C.
Scott Stevens of the
Washington Capitals

D.
Chris Chelios of the
Chicago Blackhawks

135 What is the longest wait by a living player to enter the Hall of Fame?

A. Less than 30 years

B. 30 to 40 years

C. 41 to 50 years

D. More than 50 years

136 Who in the Hall's Builder category boasts an NHL career that saw him collect more than 350 points as a player?

A.
Glen Sather

B.
Bill Hay

C.
Bud Poile

D.
Pat Quinn

133 A. The same day

A handful of elite icemen have received immediate Hall induction after retirement, but no one has ever been accorded the privilege as quickly as Dit Clapper. Prior to the opening faceoff of his last match on February 12, 1947, Clapper was showered with gifts, money and a membership scroll to the Hall of Fame, a fitting tribute to the Bruins great whose gamesmanship exceeded all but a few stars during his era. While his instant enshrinement was a product of the times, Clapper left an indelible mark as hockey's first 20-year man. He was named to multiple All-Star Teams and played on three Stanley Cup championship clubs, both as a forward and a defenseman, and with his terrific shot he delivered a career-high 41 goals in the 44-game schedule of 1929–30.

Dit Clapper

134 C. Scott Stevens of the Washington Capitals

Scott Stevens was much more than a lethal weapon of intimidation. As a measure of his overall importance to his team, by the time he retired, Stevens had played in more regular-season wins than anyone else in NHL history. Further, he never recorded a minus in the plus-minus ratings during his 22-year career, and when he won 2000's Conn Smythe Trophy as playoff MVP, Stevens scored only 11 points for the champion New Jersey Devils—a rare Smythe awarded almost exclusively for defensive play to a non-goalie. Through it all, he accrued more penalty minutes in one season than any other Hall member, led by his man-of-war 283 minutes of 1986–87. Chris Chelios is one minute back of Stevens with 282 in 1992–93. They share the top six spots in box time.

Most Regular-Season Penalty Minutes by Hall of Famers

Player	Induction Year	Team	Season	Scoring	PIM
Scott Stevens	2007	Washington	1986–87	10-51-61	283
Chris Chelios	2013	Chicago	1992–93	15-58-73	282
Chris Chelios	2013	Chicago	1991–92	9-47-56	245
Scott Stevens	2007	Washington	1988–89	7-61-68	225
Scott Stevens	2007	Washington	1984–85	21-44-65	221
Chris Chelios	2013	Chicago	1993–94	16-44-60	212
Brendan Shanahan	2013	St. Louis	1993–94	52-50-102	211
Scott Stevens	2007	Washington	1983–84	13-32-45	201

135 D. More than 50 years

This crown of thorns belongs to little-known speedster Billy McGimsie, a Stanley Cup champion center with the 1907 Kenora Thistles. The championship was McGimsie's final playoff in a six-year amateur career, all with Rat Portage/Kenora, the club he signed with in 1902 after abandoning his education and paying the team entry fee of $2. His Cup dream came true at age 26, but his next feat in hockey took a little longer: a record wait of 55 years for Hall recognition. When his induction was announced in 1962, McGimsie was 82 years old. Seven other inductees were in attendance, and another 14 deceased hockey stars received Hall crests at the 1963 ceremony. McGimsie is also among the oldest living players ever enshrined by the Hall, eclipsed by Herbie Lewis, who was 83 at 1989's Hall event. Lewis, who waited 48 years to be decorated, suited up for all three Detroit NHL teams, the Cougars, the Falcons and the Red Wings. His play was invaluable on the Wings' top line when Detroit rolled to consecutive Cups in 1936 and 1937. Lewis died in 1991 and McGimsie in 1968.

Billy McGimsie

136 B. Bill Hay

Quality players who achieve even greater success in their second careers as coaches and executives sometimes join the Hall in the Player category. Lester Patrick, Jack Adams and Dick Irvin are hockey legends of such merit. On occasion, players get elected into the Builder category—equally meritorious, as their Hall status reflects the real strengths of their game. Modern Builders Glen Sather, Brian Kilrea and Craig Patrick were marginal players whose best years came after they put away their sticks. A third and more exclusive category includes Bill Hay and Bud Poile, two Builders who proved themselves equally as players and as executives. Poile and Hay each won a Stanley Cup, Poile with Toronto in 1947 and Hay as a member of Chicago's 1961 champions. Hay, an NCAA graduate from Colorado College, scored 386 points in eight seasons with the Hawks. Retirement never meant quitting hockey for either man. Poile ran several teams and served as commissioner of the Central Hockey League and the International Hockey League, establishing the "I" as a major development league for NHL talent. Hay's distinguished résumé includes several senior executive roles, most recently with the Hockey Hall of Fame.

Most NHL Points by Hall of Fame Builders

Builder	Induction Year	NHL Career	GP	Scoring
Bill Hay	2015	1959–1967	506	113-273-386
Bud Poile	1990	1942–1950	311	107-122-229
Glen Sather	1997	1966–1976	658	80-113-193
Craig Patrick	2001	1971–1979	401	72-91-163
Pat Quinn	2016	1968–1977	606	18-113-131

137 Which Hall of Famer is the NHL's lowest draft pick to win the Calder Trophy as rookie of the year?

A.
Luc Robitaille, 1987

B.
Martin Brodeur, 1994

C.
Sergei Makarov, 1990

D.
Bryan Leetch, 1989

138 Numerous old-timers from pre-NHL days became Hall members, but among honorees with NHL experience, what is the least number of regular-season games played?

A.
One game

B.
10 to 30 games

C.
31 to 70 games

D.
More than 70 games

139 What is the least number of NHL regular-season games played by a Hall member whose professional career began in the NHL?

A. Less than 150 games

B. Between 150 and 300 games

C. Between 301 and 500 games

D. More than 500 games

140 Which Hall of Fame goalie has the worst career goals-against average?

A.
Gump Worsley

B.
Billy Smith

C.
Chuck Rayner

D.
Grant Fuhr

Sergei Makarov

137 C. Sergei Makarov, 1990

There wasn't much surprise in hockey circles over the NHL debut of Sergei Makarov. Even though he was drafted 241st overall and went on to win the Calder Trophy as top rookie, no one would call him a hidden gem: that elusive player teams hope to discover deep in late draft rounds. By the time Calgary finally got him in 1989, after waiting six years for Soviet emigration restrictions to ease, Makarov was already a nine-time winner of the Izvestia Trophy as the Soviet league's leading scorer and a winner of multiple Olympics and World Championships. The only unknown was just how quickly the 12-year veteran would adapt to North American play. Not long, as it turned out. As a member of the famed KLM Troika, with linemates Vladimir Krutov and Igor Larionov, Makarov was such a skilled play-maker that he could adjust to any system on any ice. In his first NHL season, the 31-year-old finished fourth in Flames scoring with 86 points and was named the league's top freshman. He became the Calder's lowest draft choice and its oldest player. His six-year NHL career was unremarkable by Hall standards, but it is what Makarov did at Russian and international levels that places him among the greatest players ever produced in Europe. Makarov retired in 1997.

138 A. One game

No one reaches the Hall of Fame as a one-game wonder, but two players did ascend to hockey's highest echelon by playing just a single NHL regular-season match—both hitting the ice as player substitutes. The most celebrated of this unique duo is Lester Patrick, who suited up for just one contest in 1926–27 (and another during the 1928 playoffs), each time subbing for injured players while he was managing the New York Rangers. Patrick was a hockey visionary who acted as a coach, manager, team owner, league founder and NHL governor. Like many Hall members with few NHL games under their belts, Patrick established his playing reputation in another pro league. In his case, he had played in Western circuits, where he became one of the first defensemen to routinely lead an offensive attack. He also won successive Stanley Cups with the Montreal Wanderers in 1906 and 1907. The second Hall member sporting a one-game NHL career is Barney Stanley, a Western star during the game's early years. He famously scored four goals in Vancouver's 1915 Cup win against Ottawa. Stanley played his one NHL match while coaching Chicago in 1927–28.

Lester Patrick

Fewest NHL Games by Hall of Fame Players

Player	Induction Year	Team	NHL Career	GP	Scoring
Lester Patrick	1947	NY Rangers	1926–1927	1	0-0-0
Barney Stanley	1962	Chicago	1927–1928	1	0-0-0
Art Ross	1949	Mtl. Wanderers	1917–1918	3	1-0-1
Tommy Smith	1973	Quebec	1919–1920	10	0-1-1
Harry Hyland	1962	Mtl. Wanderers, Ottawa	1917–1918	17	14-2-16
Jack Laviolette	1962	Montreal	1917–1918	18	2-1-3

139 A. Less than 150 games

Shorty Green played only four NHL seasons, but his impact on the league was seismic and still reverberates today. His play revived the struggling Hamilton Tigers, and his moral obligation cost his club a potential championship and, ultimately, forced the franchise to fold. Despite many attempts, Hamilton has never again had an NHL team. As captain of the Tigers he transformed the team from worst to first in his sophomore season of 1924–25. It was the Tigers' first postseason in their five-year history, and on the eve of those playoffs Green became a guiding force in a players' strike. "I never regretted my part in the strike, even though it cost me my chance at the Stanley Cup," Green said years later, adding "We realized hockey was becoming big. All we asked was the players be given some share of revenue." The league refused and suspended the franchise, which was then sold to New York promoters and renamed the Americans. Months later, it was Green who scored the first goal in Madison Square Garden's history. He played two more seasons, for a career total of 103 NHL games, before a serious kidney injury forced him to retire. Green never led the league in scoring, never earned an individual award or team trophy, but he won the Hall of Fame as a 1962 inductee.

Fewest NHL Games by Hall Players Who Started in the NHL

Player	Induction Year	Teams	NHL Career	GP	Scoring
Shorty Green	1962	Hamilton, NY Americans	1923–1927	103	33-20-53
Jack Adams	1959	Toronto, Ottawa	1917–1927	173	83-32-115
Babe Dye	1970	Toronto, Hamilton, Chicago, NY Americans	1919–1931	271	201-47-248
Joe Primeau	1963	Toronto	1927–1936	310	66-177-243
Gordie Drillon	1975	Toronto, Montreal	1936–1943	311	155-139-294
Ace Bailey	1975	Toronto	1926–1934	313	111-82-193

Note: Several NHLers, such as Carl Voss (261 games) and John Mariucci (223), with low game totals were elected as Builders.

140 D. Grant Fuhr

How does a goalie manage a career average of 3.38 goals-against and still find steady work for 19 years in the NHL—and then achieve Hall of Fame glory? Somehow Grant Fuhr found a way. How bad were his numbers? Fuhr registered 15 seasons with an average above 3.00, scratched out just 25 shutouts in 868 games and had an uninspiring career save percentage of .887. However, ask his Edmonton teammates, with whom he shared five Stanley Cups, and they will tell you that Fuhr was a big reason why the Oilers' run-and-gun offense worked. Edmonton became the highest-scoring team in NHL history with Fuhr as the last line of defense or, as some joked, the only line of defense. Meanwhile, he became the youngest goalie to play in an All-Star Game and the league-leader for the longest undefeated streak by a rookie (23 games). "The only statistic that matters is winning," said Fuhr, who became the Hall's first black player in his first year of eligibility, 2003.

The Highs and Lows of Goals-Against Averages*

The Hall's Highest GAAs					
Player	Induction Year	Career	GP	Record	GAA
Grant Fuhr	2003	1981–2000	868	403-295-114	3.38
Georges Vezina	1945	1917–1926	190	103-81-5	3.28
Billy Smith	1993	1971–1989	680	305-233-105	3.17
Chuck Rayner	1973	1940–1953	424	138-208-77	3.05
Tony Esposito	1988	1968–1984	886	423-306-151	2.92

The Hall's Lowest GAAs					
Player	Induction Year	Career	GP	Record	GAA
Alex Connell	1958	1924–1937	417	193-156-67	1.91
George Hainsworth	1961	1926–1937	465	246-145-74	1.93
Charlie Gardiner	1945	1927–1934	316	112-152-52	2.02
Tiny Thompson	1959	1928–1940	553	284-194-75	2.08
Dominik Hasek	2014	1990–2008	735	389-223-95	2.20

*Minimum of 150 games

141
What is the most NHL trades racked up by a Hall of Famer?

A.
Five trades

B.
Seven trades

C.
Nine trades

D.
11 trades

142
Which NHL 500-goal scorer waited the longest for Hall recognition after his retirement?

A.
Michel Goulet

B.
Dino Ciccarelli

C.
Bryan Trottier

D.
Dale Hawerchuk

143

What was the longest gap between retirement and induction for a Hall of Famer?

A. Less than 60 years

B. Between 60 and 70 years

C. Between 71 and 80 years

D. More than 80 years

144

Who coached the most NHL games after becoming an honored member of the Hall of Fame?

A.
Scotty Bowman

B.
Al Arbour

C.
Roger Neilson

D.
Glen Sather

141 B. **Seven trades**

It's safe to say that Mike Sillinger, Brent Ashton and Jeff Norton aren't on anyone's short list for Hall enshrinement. As some of the most traveled NHLers, there is a slim-to-none chance of their being nominated. However, the next player on the NHL's list of most-traded players is a Hall of Famer. This guy would have been enshrined after his first team and trade—regardless of his efforts during the rest of his 21-year career. Paul Coffey was that good on the Edmonton Oilers. He won multiple Norris Trophies as the league's top defenseman, numerous First and Second All-Star Team berths, three Stanley Cups and scored 48 goals in 1985–86, eclipsing Bobby Orr's record of 46 by a rearguard. Then, a contract dispute pushed the Oilers to deal him to Pittsburgh, the first of seven trades and one free-agent signing, which brought Coffey to another eight clubs. He got a fourth Cup in 1991 and won more silverware and All-Star appearances, but the Edmonton years secured Coffey's Hall of Fame candidacy.

Paul Coffey

142 B. Dino Ciccarelli

Hockey's most exclusive club of goal getters seldom sees any of its members wait beyond the Hall's mandatory three-year period. Typically, 500-goal scorers gain entry on their first try. Then again, this is Dino Ciccarelli, a player who wasn't even considered talented enough for an NHL draft. And when he did make it, he failed to garner any major NHL individual or team awards and never earned an All-Star berth, and his maverick ways caused several run-ins with both players and the law. But Ciccarelli had a big-league knack for offense, particularly on the man-advantage in front of the net, where he scored 232 power-play goals of his career 608 goals. It remains the highest goal count by a draft-eligible player who was never selected. Ciccarelli could score during postseason play too. He made geniuses of Minnesota management in 1981, when he popped in an NHL rookie-record 14 goals in 19 playoff games for the North Stars, a league mark that still stands today. Further, the sparkplug winger is the first NHLer to score playoff hat tricks with three different teams: Minnesota, Washington and Detroit between 1981 and 1993. In a career without regrets, Ciccarelli carried a lot of baggage into retirement. He cooled his heels until 2010, eight years after his eligibility. But he kept good company with 500-goal scorers Pat Verbeek, Pierre Turgeon and Dave Andreychuk—none have to date received Hall admittance.

143 B. Between 60 and 70 years

This answer involves some obscure yet fascinating old-timers. When the Hall of Fame began venerating several overlooked players during the 1960s, the honorees were often trailblazers. Some were enshrined posthumously, among them Jack Marshall, a six-time Stanley Cup champion on a record four different teams in pre-NHL play. Marshall waited nearly a half-century for his call to the Hall after retiring in 1917. Sadly, he died only three weeks before being enshrined in August 1965. He was 88 years old. Two other alumni from Marshall's 1965 Hall class were linemates Fred Scanlan and Arthur Farrell of the Montreal Shamrocks. Along with rover Harry Trihey, Scanlan and Farrell revolutionized the forward line, favoring what Frank Selke called "the new-style combination attacks" of deft line-passing over the traditional individual play of solo rushes. Scanlan's Hall accolade took 62 years, and Farrell's took a record 64 years, the longest interval between retirement and induction by any Hall member, although neither man was alive to receive his long-overdue reward.

Arthur Farrell

144 A. Scotty Bowman

The Stanley Cup just seems to follow some people around—even as Hall members. At his 1991 induction, Scotty Bowman's coaching days appeared over. His last bench duties had ended four years earlier with Buffalo, where he left the game as the winningest coach in NHL play. However, Bowman was lured back as Pittsburgh's director of player personnel in 1990 and soon took over the reins with the untimely death of Penguins coach Bob Johnson. Under Bowman, Pittsburgh repeated as Stanley Cup champions in 1992, a season dedicated to Johnson. Remarkably, this was his first of another four Cups while wearing his Hall ring. He also added 505 wins, more than 40 percent of his NHL-record haul of 1,244 victories. With nothing left to win, Bowman quit the bench in 2002, boasting an imposing .657 win percentage during a 30-year career. His nine Stanley Cups as a coach rank first all-time, with almost half won as a Hall member.

The Stanley Cup Charm of Scotty Bowman

Coaching Career (1967–2002)							
Regular Season				Playoffs			
Team	GC	W-L-O/T	PTS %	GC	W-L	W-L %	Cups
St. Louis	238	110-83-45	.557	52	26–26	.500	Lost final in 1968, 1969, 1970
Montreal	634	419-110-105	.744	98	70–28	.714	Won in 1973, 1976, 1977, 1978, 1979
Buffalo	404	210-134-60	.594	36	18–18	.500	Best result: Lost semifinal
Pittsburgh	164	95-53-16	.628	33	23–10	.697	Won in 1992
Detroit	701	410-193-98	.655	134	86–48	.642	Won in 1997, 1998, 2002; lost final in 1995
Total	2141	1244-573-324	.657	353	223–130	.632	9 Cups

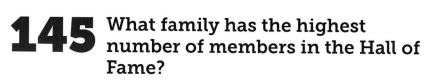

The Howes

145

What family has the highest number of members in the Hall of Fame?

A. The Howes

B. The Hulls

C. The Patricks

D. The Conachers

146 What is the highest number of NHL games played by an individual in the Hall's Builder category?

A. Less than 100 games

B. Between 100 and 250 games

C. Between 251 and 500 games

D. More than 500 games

147 The Hall of Fame's longest surviving member was how old in 2017?

A. Less than 90 years old

B. Between 90 and 95 years old

C. Between 96 and 100 years old

D. More than 100 years old

148 Who is the Hall member with the fewest number of penalty minutes collected in an NHL career of 300 games or more (excluding goalies)?

A.
Clint Smith

B.
Buddy O'Connor

C.
Bobby Bauer

D.
Edgar Laprade

145 C. The Patricks

There isn't another hockey family who has contributed more to the improvement and quality of the game than the Patrick dynasty. Some members had great skill, while others were merely ordinary, but each first developed a view of the game from center ice out as a player. Brothers Lester and Frank played hockey in Montreal before moving to British Columbia, where they built Canada's first artificial rinks, painted the first blue lines for offside calls and introduced the penalty shot and the playoff format. As the game grew, one generation of Patricks succeeded the other, both on the ice and behind the scenes. Lester's sons Lynn and Muzz played, coached and served as general managers in the NHL, as did Lester's grandson, Craig, who perpetuated his family's legacy as a longtime manager of the Pittsburgh Penguins. Three generations of Patricks produced four Hall of Famers, with Lester and Lynn elected in the Player category and Frank and Craig as Builders, the most honorees from one family (the Conachers are a close second with three). If hockey has a royal family, it's the Patricks.

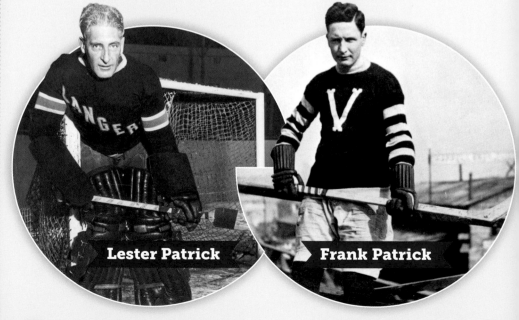

Lester Patrick

Frank Patrick

Glen Sather

146 D. More than 500 games

There is a compelling story of achievement for each of the dozen-plus players in the Hall's Builder category—their fame coming from their off-ice contributions. Al Arbour had the most Cup success among this group of hockey-playing Builders, but his 626 games can't match Glen Sather, who went Cup-less in 658 matches. Each won four Stanley Cups as coaches, Arbour running the New York Islanders and Sather as Edmonton's coach, general manager and president before he took over the New York Rangers.

Most NHL Games Played by Hall of Fame Builders

Builder	Induction Year	NHL Career	GP	Scoring
Glen Sather	1997	1966–1976	658	80-113-193
Al Arbour	1996	1953–1971	626	12-58-70
Pat Quinn	2016	1968–1977	606	18-113-131
Bill Hay	2015	1959–1967	506	113-273-386
Craig Patrick	2001	1971–1979	401	72-91-163

147 C. Between 96 and 100 years old

A few old-timers are proving that today's 90 may be the new 80 or even 70. The great Fred Taylor, whose legendary scoring and skating prowess won him hockey's famous Cyclone moniker, lived until he was almost 95 years old. Taylor may have been the game's original dangler, with the puck artistry of Pavel Datsyuk and other modern stick tricksters. It was said that he could skate backward quicker than any player on the ice could skate forward, and his ingenuity with the puck was equal to his foot speed. He once vowed to score a goal backward and then, as the story goes, embarrassed Ottawa by netting one exactly that way in March 1910. Although Taylor never played in the NHL, he did win two Stanley Cups before the league's formation in 1917. Honored in 1947, he was just weeks shy of his 95th birthday when he passed away in 1979. Taylor has since been eclipsed by other nonagenarians, including Original Six stars Milt Schmidt and Elmer Lach, both of whom became the longest living Hall of Famers at age 97 in 2015. Sadly, Lach passed that year, followed by Schmidt, the oldest member at 98, in January 2017.

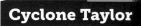

Cyclone Taylor

148 A. Clint Smith

Center Clint Smith must have had trouble locating the penalty box on the rare occasion he was assessed an infraction. During an 11-year NHL career, from 1936–37 to 1946–47, he never accumulated more than six penalty minutes in any season and had three complete seasons without a single call against him. A five-time nominee for the Lady Byng Trophy, Smith won it twice while logging only 24 penalty minutes in 483 career games, but his playmaking is what really charmed the Hall of Fame. He scored top-10 finishes in assists on four occasions, highlighted by a league-record 49 helpers in 1943–44's 50-game schedule. In later years, staying out of the sin bin proved a wise decision health-wise. While Smith was only inducted in 1991—some 39 years after his retirement—he lived into his nineties, the last surviving member of the 1940 Stanley Cup–winning New York Rangers.

The Choirboys of the Hall of Fame*

Player	Induction Year	Career	GP	PIM	Average No. of Games Between 2-min. Minors
Clint Smith	1991	1936–1947	483	24	40.25
Buddy O'Connor	1988	1941–1951	509	34	29.94
Bobby Bauer	1996	1936–1952	327	36	18.17
Edgar Laprade	1993	1945–1955	500	42	23.81
Syl Apps	1961	1936–1948	423	56	15.11
Gordie Drillon	1975	1936–1943	311	56	11.11

*Minimum 300-game career

Note: Players such as Dave Keon and Bill Quackenbush registered comparable averages, but they had longer NHL careers and, consequently, had higher minute totals.

149 What is the oldest age at which a Hall of Famer first learned to skate?

A.
10 years old

B.
12 years old

C.
14 years old

D.
16 years old

150 How often has the Hall's selection committee enshrined only one player in an induction year?

A. Only once, Wayne Gretzky in 1999

B. Two times

C. Six times

D. 10 times

151 Which 1,000-point NHLer waited the longest for his Hall induction?

A.
Bernie Federko

B.
Doug Gilmour

C.
Phil Housley

D.
Glenn Anderson

152 What is the longest time a player has remained a surviving member of the Hall of Fame?

A. Less than 40 years

B. Between 40 and 50 years

C. Between 51 and 60 years

D. More than 60 years

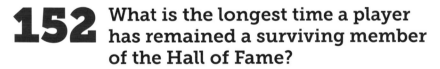

149 D. 16 years old

There is no research to definitively conclude that Lionel Conacher started skating later than any other Hall member, but few players from any hockey era ever turned pro after first strapping on blades at age 16, never mind going on to scale hockey's highest pinnacle. But Conacher was no ordinary competitor. By the time his NHL career was gearing up, through his athletic prowess and relentless drive to win, he had earned a Canadian light-heavyweight boxing title, a 27–0 record as an amateur wrestler, Canadian football's Grey Cup (in 1921), a Triple-A baseball championship (in 1926) and an Ontario senior title in lacrosse (in 1927). In sports parlance, Conacher was a natural. Because there was more money in hockey, he joined the NHL at age 24, even though it wasn't his best sport or his first passion. Fortunately, he was so gifted that his late start— about 10 years after most Canadian boys have started skating—never stopped him from realizing his greatest success, as a Hall of Fame defenseman.

Lionel Conacher

150 B. Two times

Wayne Gretzky did so much for the game and set so many records that comparisons rarely seem appropriate or fair. However, one star pivot from the 1940s does share some intriguing statistics with the Great One. Similar to Gretzky, Bill Cowley was a playmaker with elite vision, and for a few years his domination of hockey was nearly on a par with No. 99. When Gretzky recorded one more assist than anyone else's point total in 1982–83, the only other player who had achieved that kind of success was Cowley, with Boston in 1940–41. That season, the Bruins center ruled the NHL scoring race with 62 points after racking up 45 assists—one more than the next highest point total (44). And when Gretzky set a new points-per-game average of 2.05 in 1980–81, whose mark did he break? Cowley's 1.97, established in 1943–44. Cowley potted 71 points in 36 games, while Gretzky had 164 points in 80 matches. Certainly Cowley was no Gretzky, but both men share the Hall exclusive of being the only players enshrined in their induction year: Cowley in 1968 and Gretzky in 1999.

Bill Cowley

Crazy or What? Bill Cowley and Wayne Gretzky: More Assists Than Runner-up Points

1940–41 NHL Season			1982–83 NHL Season		
Lead Scorers	GP	Stats	Lead Scorers	GP	Stats
Bill Cowley	46	17-**45**-62	Wayne Gretzky	80	71-**125**-196
Bryan Hextall	48	26-18-**44**	Peter Stastny	75	47-77-**124**
Gordie Drillon	42	23-21-**44**	Denis Savard	78	35-86-121
Syl Apps	41	20-24-**44**	Mike Bossy	79	60-58-118

151 A. Bernie Federko

Despite all the 1,000-point players, most millennium men make the Hall, often on their first try. However, for every Ray Bourque and Mats Sundin, there are bubble players, such as Glenn Anderson and Phil Housley, who only got elected after nine-year purgatorial stints. Meanwhile, it took Bernie Federko 10 tries from his year of eligibility, 1993, to his 2002 induction. Federko was an unselfish scoring star who had superb passing skills and leadership qualities, but he skated in the long shadow of superstars Wayne Gretzky and Steve Yzerman. He also played on blue-collar teams in St. Louis, where he got a lot of ice time, often playing on two lines in a season. His point totals skyrocketed as a result, and during 14 years he registered four 100-point seasons, seven 30-goal seasons and 50 assists in 10 consecutive seasons, an NHL first. Federko retired with 1,130 points.

Milt Schmidt

152 C. Between 51 and 60 years

Boston's Milt Schmidt celebrated his 55th year as a Hall of Famer in 2016, before his passing just days into 2017, easily the longest tenure by a Hall member and the first honoree to mark a golden anniversary at the institution. Inducted in 1961, Schmidt was one of hockey's finest centermen while playing on the Bruins' "Kraut Line." In 1939–40, the 21-year-old led all scorers in assists and points with an Art Ross-winning 22-30-52 record. He was named a First All-Star, his first of three during a 16-year career with Boston. Schmidt retired partway through 1954–55 to coach the Bruins, where he stayed until assuming manager duties in 1967. His rebuild began immediately with several key moves to complement the talents of Bobby Orr and, at the same time, inject toughness into his lineup. The result was hockey's most feared scoring machine of the era, adding Phil Esposito, Ken Hodge and Fred Stanfield in a heist from Chicago that remains the most important player transaction in club history. After Schmidt, Ted Lindsay was the second Hall member to celebrate 50 years in 2016. Elmer Lach had a 49-year residency at hockey's famous temple.

A Big Deal

●●

The trade of Wayne Gretzky in 1988 proved that no individual is untouchable, including the world's best player and a future Hall honoree. In this matching columns game, pick the aspiring Hall of Famers dealt for each other at various times in their memorable careers. In a few cases, some transactions involved three Hall members, the highest number of future inductees ever traded in any NHL swap.

For solutions, turn the page.

Part 1

1.	1989: Adam Oates, Detroit	A. Jarome Iginla, Dallas
2.	1994: Mike Gartner, NY Rangers	B. Newsy Lalonde, Montreal
3.	1957: Terry Sawchuk, Boston	C. Bernie Federko, St. Louis
4.	1947: Max Bentley, Chicago	D. Glenn Anderson, Toronto
5.	1995: Joe Nieuwendyk, Calgary	E. Bud Poile, Toronto
6.	1922: Aurèle Joliat, Saskatoon*	F. Johnny Bucyk, Detroit

*Rights traded away (WCHL)

Part 2

1.	1934: Howie Morenz, Montreal	A. Chris Chelios, Montreal
2.	1995: Brendan Shanahan, St. Louis	B. Andy Bathgate, NY Rangers
3.	1936: Earl Seibert, NY Rangers	C. Lionel Conacher, Chicago
4.	1990: Denis Savard, Chicago	D. Dino Ciccarelli, Minnesota
5.	1964: Dick Duff, Toronto	E. Chris Pronger, Hartford
6.	1990: Mike Gartner & Larry Murphy, Washington	F. Art Coulter, Chicago

Part 3

1.	1963: Jacques Plante, Montreal	A. Gump Worsley, NY Rangers
2.	1991: Scott Stevens, St. Louis*	B. Hooley Smith, Ottawa
3.	1933: Carl Voss, Detroit	C. Phil Esposito, Boston
4.	1927: Punch Broadbent, Mtl. Maroons	D. Sweeney Schriner, NY Americans
5.	1939: Busher Jackson, Toronto	E. Brendan Shanahan, New Jersey
6.	1975: Brad Park & Jean Ratelle, NY Rangers	F. Cooney Weiland, Ottawa

*Transferred as compensation

Part 4

1.	1968: Frank Mahovlich, Toronto	A. Paul Coffey, Detroit
2.	1953: Johnny Bower, Cleveland (AHL)	B. Frank Fredrickson, Boston
3.	1928: Mickey MacKay, Pittsburgh	C. Norm Ullman, Detroit
4.	1965: Andy Bathgate, Toronto	D. Allan Stanley, NY Rangers
5.	1954: Bill Gadsby, Chicago	E. Emile Francis, NY Rangers
6.	1996: Brendan Shanahan, Hartford	F. Marcel Pronovost, Detroit

A Big Deal
Solutions

Part 1

1. 1989: Adam Oates, Detroit   C. Bernie Federko, St. Louis
2. 1994: Mike Gartner, NY Rangers   D. Glenn Anderson, Toronto
3. 1957: Terry Sawchuk, Boston   F. Johnny Bucyk, Detroit
4. 1947: Max Bentley, Chicago   E. Bud Poile, Toronto
5. 1995: Joe Nieuwendyk, Calgary   A. Jarome Iginla, Dallas
6. 1922: Aurèle Joliat, Saskatoon   B. Newsy Lalonde, Montreal

Part 2

1. 1934: Howie Morenz, Montreal   C. Lionel Conacher, Chicago
2. 1995: Brendan Shanahan, St. Louis E. Chris Pronger, Hartford
3. 1936: Earl Seibert, NY Rangers   F. Art Coulter, Chicago
4. 1990: Denis Savard, Chicago   A. Chris Chelios, Montreal
5. 1964: Dick Duff, Toronto   B. Andy Bathgate, NY Rangers
6. 1990: Mike Gartner & Larry Murphy, D. Dino Ciccarelli, Minnesota
   Washington

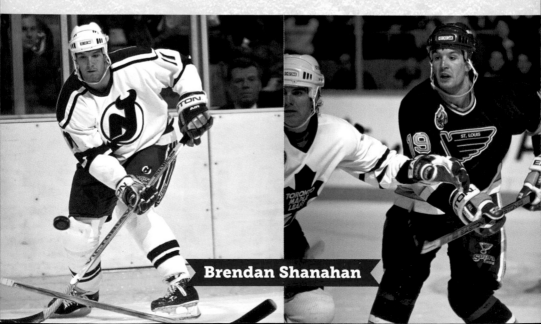

Brendan Shanahan

Part 3

Part 4

Ray Bourque and Joe Sakic

Grail Trail

What are the odds of a Stanley Cup champion making it to the Hall of Fame or a Cup-winning goal scorer getting inducted? What about the NHL's greatest comeback goalie—is he in the Hall? We can tell you that among the more than 250 players enshrined, an overwhelming majority have their names on the Cup. In fact, more than 200 have won hockey's Holy Grail. Still, if the class of 2013 is any indication—of four inductees only Joe Sakic reached Cup fame—it's what you leave on the ice that truly matters. In this chapter, we showcase the celebrated few who have captured the game's two most coveted prizes.

Questions 153-156

153 Who was the first European-born Hall of Famer to captain an NHL Stanley Cup champion team?

A. A defenseman from Sweden

B. A center from Russia

C. A winger from Finland

D. A goalie from Scotland

154 Who won the most combined Stanley Cups as a player and coach?

A.
Toe Blake

B.
Al Arbour

C.
Jacques Lemaire

D.
Red Kelly

155

Which Hall of Fame member won the Stanley Cup in the fewest number of regular-season games from the start of an NHL career?

A.
Jack Adams of the
Toronto Arenas

B.
Henri Richard of the
Montreal Canadiens

C.
Patrick Roy of the
Montreal Canadiens

D.
Marcel Pronovost of the
Detroit Red Wings

156

What ratio of NHLers who score a Stanley Cup–winning goal make it into the Hall of Fame?

A. Only one in every four Cup–winning scorers

B. About one in every three Cup–winning scorers

C. About one in every two Cup–winning scorers

D. About two in every three Cup–winning scorers

Charlie Gardiner

153 D. A goalie from Scotland

Future Hall of Fame candidate Nicklas Lidstrom is the first European-trained Stanley Cup captain, but 74 years before the Swedish rearguard drank from Lord Stanley's jug in 2008, goalie Charlie Gardiner captained Chicago to the 1934 championship. Born in Edinburgh, Scotland, Gardiner settled in Canada at age 7 and fell in love with hockey. His inferior skating skills forced him to play in net, where he developed into a fearless puckstopper who routinely challenged rushing forwards for the puck. Gardiner's brilliance kept the woeful Black Hawks in contention, especially in 1933–34, when the team's popgun offense netted the league's worst goal count. Despite its lack of attack, Chicago finished third overall in the nine-team NHL, as Gardiner led all goalies with 10 shutouts and had a stunning 1.63 goals-against average. In the playoffs, the Hawks' crease captain shut down Montreal and then held off Detroit in the best-of-five final, stoning the Wings 1–0 in a dramatic 30-minute overtime Cup winner. Gardiner's captaincy lasted one season. He died unexpectedly months after his Cup victory.

154 A. Toe Blake

As a player and coach, no individual won like Toe Blake. Between the two jobs, he captured 11 Stanley Cups, with three championships skating for Montreal's Maroons and Canadiens and another eight coaching the Habs, including an NHL-record five in a row from 1956 to 1960. Blake put what he learned as a leader on the ice into practice behind the bench. Tough and demanding, he made his best players better because, as former Habs often said, Blake didn't know what the word "lose" meant, because it wasn't in his vocabulary. Jacques Lemaire won nine Cups as a player and coach and one more title in a team management role for the 1993 Canadiens.

Most Combined Stanley Cups by a Player-Turned-Coach

Player	Induction Year	Cups as a Player	Cups as a Coach	Total
Toe Blake	1966	3 (Mtl. Maroons, 1935; Montreal, 1944, 1946)	8 (Montreal, 1956–1960, 1965, 1966, 1968)	11
Jacques Lemaire	1984	8 (Montreal, 1968, 1969, 1971, 1973, 1976–1979)	1 (New Jersey, 1995)	9
Al Arbour	1996	4 (Detroit, 1954; Chicago, 1961; Toronto, 1962, 1964)	4 (NY Islanders, 1980–1983)	8
Larry Robinson	1995	6 (Montreal, 1973, 1976–1979, 1986)	1 (New Jersey, 2000)	7
Tom Johnson	1970	6 (Montreal, 1953, 1956–1960)	1 (Boston, 1972)	7
Hap Day	1961	1 (Toronto, 1932)	5 (Toronto, 1942, 1945 1947–1949)	6

155 D. Marcel Pronovost
of the Detroit Red Wings

It may be the most schizoid combo of records owned by a Stanley Cup champion. Marcel Pronovost logged the shortest regular season before winning the Cup by a future Hall of Famer and, 53 years later, happened to chart the longest stretch between the first and last time any individual had his name etched in silver. Pronovost was just 19 years old when he replaced Red Kelly on Detroit's blue line during the 1950 postseason. Nine games later the Red Wings won it all and Pronovost was sipping champagne— without a single NHL regular-season game to his credit. He retired in 1970 with four more Cups. Soon, he was coaching junior hockey and, later, scouting for New Jersey when the Devils won the Cup in 1995, 2000 and 2003. It was a league mark of more than a half-century after his first taste of the championship as a wide-eyed rookie in 1950.

Marcel Pronovost

Bill Barilko

156 C. About one in every two Cup–winning scorers

Almost 100 Stanley Cup winners have been recorded since NHL playoffs began in 1918, and for every Bobby Orr, Mark Messier and Brett Hull in the Hall there is a Darren McCarty, Uwe Krupp and Ulf Samuelsson—three players among more than 40 Cup-winning goal scorers eligible for induction who are without a Hall of Fame credit. Other Cup scorers not in the Hall include such famous names as Bill Barilko, who potted Toronto's winner in 1951, Bob Nystrom of the 1980 New York Islanders and Kirk Muller of the 1993 Montreal Canadiens.

157 What is the highest goals-per-game average by an NHL playoff performer in one season?

A. 1.00 goals per game

B. 1.30 goals per game

C. 1.70 goals per game

D. 2.00 goals per game

158 Which Hall of Famer is the only NHLer to play all six positions in a Stanley Cup playoff series?

A.
King Clancy of the Ottawa Senators

B.
Tim Horton of the
Toronto Maple Leafs

C.
Allan Stanley of the
New York Rangers

D.
Guy Lapointe of the
Montreal Canadiens

159 What playoff feat is exclusive to Hall of Famers Mike Bossy and old-timer Jack Darragh?

A. They each recorded the most playoff goals in one game

B. They each set record point-scoring streaks in one playoff

C. They each potted the fastest goal from the start of a game

D. They each scored consecutive Stanley Cup winners

160 Which Hall of Famer logged the most consecutive years in the playoffs without winning a Stanley Cup?

A.
Borje Salming

B.
Brad Park

C.
Mark Howe

D.
Bill Gadsby

157 C. 1.70 goals per game

Newsy Lalonde

The 1919 Stanley Cup playoffs are remembered mostly for being canceled. Several players were hospitalized with influenza, one of whom later died. However, out of the tragedy of that doomed postseason another story emerged, one authored by the fabled Newsy Lalonde. Early hockey's most colorful iceman, Lalonde was a born leader and a fierce fighter, sporting a temper that no one escaped, not opponents, spectators or even apathetic teammates. And he could outscore almost anyone on the ice on any given night. During the 1919 playoffs, Lalonde caught fire and potted 11 goals in Montreal's series win against Ottawa, including the first five-goal game in playoff history, and then he added six more in five games during the abandoned Cup Final against Seattle. That final round was suspended with no winner declared, but Lalonde established an NHL mark that still stands today by netting a 1.70 average with 17 goals in 10 matches, the highest single postseason mark ever.

Highest Goals-per-Game Average in One Playoff Year*

Player	Induction Year	Team	Year	Goals	GP	Avg.
Newsy Lalonde	1950	Montreal	1919	17	10	1.70
Babe Dye	1970	Toronto	1922	11	7	1.57
Maurice Richard	1961	Montreal	1944	12	9	1.33
Jean Béliveau	1972	Montreal	1956	12	10	1.20
Reggie Leach		Philadelphia	1976	19	16	1.19
Lanny McDonald	1992	Toronto	1977	10	9	1.11

*Minimum of two series in a playoff year

158 A. King Clancy of the Ottawa Senators

"Battered to pieces" was how Ottawa manager Tommy Gorman described his nine-player squad that confronted the speedy Edmonton Eskimos at the 1923 Stanley Cup Final. With six regulars and three subs, including defenseman King Clancy, the Senators had battled through two rounds before their best-of-three Cup Final. In Ottawa's two hard-fought victories against Edmonton for the championship, Gorman played Clancy in every skating position, having him replace injured rearguards George Boucher (cut foot) and Eddie Gerard (dislocated shoulder) and left winger Cy Denneny (bruised leg), as well as exhausted center Frank Nighbor and right winger Punch Broadbent. Then, in the second period of Cup-winning Game 2, Sens goalie Clint Benedict drew a two-minute penalty for slashing Joe Simpson and was forced to serve it in the box, as was the custom in old-time hockey. Out skated Gorman's steady substitute Clancy, who blocked several shots, including one where he "dropped his stick, caught the puck with the skill of a baseball catcher, and turned it aside," according to game reports. The 1923 series made Clancy a star and established his "unique record of filling, during the series, every position on the team," said Gorman.

159 D. They each scored consecutive Stanley Cup winners

The Stanley Cup heroics of Jack Darragh and Mike Bossy are bound by some curious similarities even though they are 62 years apart. Both men played right wing, although Darragh, one of the NHL's first off-wing forwards, shot left. Both of their first Cup winners, Darragh's in 1920 with the Ottawa Senators and Bossy's in 1982 with the New York Islanders, were scored at exactly 5:00 into a period, and each was their team's second goal in 6–1 and 3–1 victories, respectively. Both goals also came against West Coast teams, Ottawa playing against Seattle and the Islanders against Vancouver. Both men won four Stanley Cups and all with the same team, Darragh as a Senator and Bossy on Long Island. No other NHL players have ever notched back-to-back Cup winners. Darragh's second winner came in 1921 and Bossy's in 1983.

Jack Darragh

Mike Bossy

160 B. Brad Park

Few NHL stars had worse timing than Brad Park. He entered the league just as Bobby Orr was making the Norris Trophy part of his permanent collection. Then, after Orr, Park played bridesmaid to Denis Potvin for a total of six runner-up Norris finishes. And Park wasn't any luckier with playoff silverware. He played 17 seasons on ravaged knees and qualified every playoff year, first skating in seven postseasons for the New York Rangers then eight playoffs with Boston, followed by two more with Detroit. Yet he never won a championship. Every eligible player with Park's playoff longevity has gone to the Hall of Fame, including Park, but he is the only one among that select group of stars without a Stanley Cup.

Most Consecutive Years in Playoffs

Player	Induction Year	Teams	Playoff Career	Years	Cups
Larry Robinson	1995	Montreal, Los Angeles	1973–1992	20	6
Nicklas Lidstrom	2015	Detroit	1992–2012*	20	4
Brett Hull	2009	Calgary, St. Louis, Dallas, Detroit	1986–2004	19	2
Larry Murphy	2004	Washington, Minnesota, Pittsburgh, Toronto, Detroit	1984–2001	18	4
Brad Park	1988	NY Rangers, Boston, Detroit	1969–1985	17	0
Ray Bourque	2004	Boston	1980–1996	17	1**
Kris Draper	Eligible in 2014	Detroit	1994–2011*	17	4

* Except lockout year, 2004–05

**Ray Bourque's Cup came with Colorado in 2001

161 What NHL playoff feat is attributed to little-known general manager Tommy Gorman?

A. Gorman won Stanley Cups with the most NHL franchises

B. Gorman won the most consecutive Stanley Cups

C. Gorman won Stanley Cups with the most non-NHL franchises

D. Gorman won a Stanley Cup as a manager before winning it as a player

162 Which Hall of Famer netted the most NHL regular-season points without winning the Stanley Cup?

A.
Gilbert Perreault

B.
Peter Stastny

C.
Marcel Dionne

D.
Pat LaFontaine

163 How many of the 16 players who scored Stanley Cup winners in overtime have become Hall members?

A. Only two overtime Cup scorers have become Hall of Famers

B. Eight overtime Cup scorers have become Hall of Famers

C. 12 overtime Cup scorers have become Hall of Famers

D. All 16 overtime Cup scorers have become Hall of Famers

164 Which two individuals won the most Stanley Cups after being inducted into the Hall of Fame?

A.
Jean Béliveau and Scotty Bowman

B.
Scotty Bowman and Toe Blake

C.
Toe Blake and Jacques Lemaire

D.
Jacques Lemaire and Jean Béliveau

161 A. Gorman won Stanley Cups with the most NHL franchises

No general manager had more success at turning teams into Stanley Cup champions than Tommy Gorman. He didn't capture the most Cups, but like the man who did, coach Scotty Bowman, almost everywhere Gorman went he won. Gorman even eclipsed icons Conn Smythe and Jack Adams, who never won as consistently with as many clubs. After turning Ottawa into the NHL's first dynasty with Cups in 1920, 1921 and 1923, Gorman helped popularize hockey in New York with the city's first team, the Americans. Then he produced an NHL wonder, claiming back-to-back titles with different clubs, as manager and coach of the 1934 Chicago Black Hawks and the 1935 Montreal Maroons. He later crossed the street and took the Canadiens to two Cups, in 1944 and 1946. Gorman's final tally? He built seven Stanley Cup champions with four different franchises. His entry into the Hall's Builder category came in 1963.

Tommy Gorman

Answ

163 B

162 C.
Marcel Dionne

The top-10 list of NHLers who didn't win the Stanley Cup includes Hall of Famers Pat LaFontaine, Peter Stastny and Mike Gartner, but first place in this Cup-less group of elite marksmen belongs to the best player never crowned champion, Marcel Dionne. Other titles came his way, notably NHL scoring champion in 1979–80, but his 1,771-point career never got Dionne's teams past the second playoff round in 18 seasons with Detroit, Los Angeles and the New York Rangers, and on eight occasions his teams failed to make the postseason entirely.

Eight overtime Cup scorers have become Hall of Famers

Victory doesn't come any sweeter than one shot on net clinching the whole season. It just doesn't guarantee the Hall of Fame. In fact, half of the 16 NHLers with an overtime Cup winner have not been enshrined, including Detroit's Pete Babando (1950) and Tony Leswick (1954), both of whom delivered Cups to the Red Wings in the most pressure-packed situation, a Game 7 sudden-death overtime.

Bryan Hextall

The Overtime Stanley Cup Winners of the Hall of Fame

Player	Induction Year	Team	Year	OT Time	Score	Series
Brett Hull	2009	Dallas	1999	54:51	2–1	4–2
Jacques Lemaire	1984	Montreal	1977	4:32	2–1	4–0
Bobby Orr	1979	Boston	1970	0:40	4–3	4–0
Henri Richard	1979	Montreal	1966	2:20	3–2	4–2
Elmer Lach	1966	Montreal	1953	1:22	1–0	4–1
Toe Blake	1966	Montreal	1944	9:12	5–4	4–0
Bryan Hextall	1969	NY Rangers	1940	2:07	3–2	4–2
Bill Cook	1952	NY Rangers	1933	7:34	1–0	3–1

164 A. Jean Béliveau and Scotty Bowman

Scotty Bowman's name usually figures prominently anytime there's a roll call of big Stanley Cup winners. On numbers alone, Bowman was more successful after becoming a Hall member in 1991. A six-time champion prior to his induction, he acquired another seven afterward, through his coaching and club management posts with Pittsburgh, Detroit and Chicago. After Jean Béliveau's retirement in 1971 and his Hall induction in 1972, the 10-time Cup winner added seven more titles while in senior administrative roles with the Canadiens. Both men won seven Cups as Hall of Famers.

165

Who is the only Hall of Famer to participate in 100 playoff games both as a player and as a head coach in the NHL?

A.
Toe Blake

B.
Al Arbour

C.
Bob Pulford

D.
Jacques Lemaire

166

What is the highest number of future Hall of Fame players on a Stanley Cup team?

A. Nine players

B. 11 players

C. 13 players

D. 15 players

167 How many Stanley Cup champion teams do not have a player represented in the Hall of Fame?

A. None, every Cup winner has had one of its players inducted

B. Only two teams

C. Six teams

D. 12 teams

168 Which Hall of Fame coach won Builder honors while setting an NHL record for most playoff games coached without winning the Stanley Cup?

A.
Roger Neilson

B.
Emile Francis

C.
Pat Quinn

D.
Lou Lamoriello

165 D. Jacques Lemaire

Few old-time players or coaches ever accumulated enough playoff series to top the 100-game mark because, for many years, a trip to the Stanley Cup Final meant only two rounds in a best-of-seven format. For all his success, Toe Blake played only 58 playoff matches and coached 119 to net his record 11 Stanley Cups. However, the advent of three- and four-round postseasons, beginning with expansion in 1967–68, meant players and a few coaches could amass game totals in the triple-digits. So how many individuals managed such a combination of Cup luck? Our research found only one: Jacques Lemaire. Ironically, the former two-way center-turned-bench boss coached the trap, a defensive strategy that ran contrary to the fire-wagon hockey he played so effectively with Montreal in the 1970s. Lemaire skated in 145 playoff games and directed another 117 matches, winning a combined nine championships. His Hall call came in 1984.

Most Playoff Games by a Hall Player-Turned-Coach

Player	Induction Year	Player GP	Coach GC	Total	Cups
Al Arbour	1996	86	209	295	8
Larry Robinson	1995	227	52	279	7
Jacques Lemaire	1984	145	117	262	9
Bob Gainey	1992	182	54	236	5
Red Kelly	1969	164	62	226	8
Wayne Gretzky	1999	208	0	208	4
Glen Sather	1997	72	127	199	4
Pat Quinn	2016	11	183	194	0

Note: Chicago's Joel Quenneville has more than 230 games and counting.

166 B. 11 players

Quelle surprise! None of Montreal's three Stanley Cup dynasties iced the greatest collection of Hall of Famers on one championship team. That distinction belongs to the powerhouse squad of 21 regulars on the 1973 Canadiens, who straddled the Habs dynasties of the 1960s and late-1970s but produced 11 future Hall members. Every player position was represented, including two entire scoring lines, the top-four defensemen and a goalie. Throughout the 1980s almost every Hall class had a member of the 1973 champion Canadiens. The team was also managed by future Hall members: head coach Scotty Bowman, general manager Sam Pollock and vice president Jean Béliveau, a 1972 inductee. The Cup-winning 1956 Canadiens and 1967 Toronto Maple Leafs each yielded 10 Hall members.

Yvan Cournoyer

The 14 Hall of Famers of the 1973 Montreal Canadiens

Player	Induction Year	Position	Player	Induction Year	Position
Henri Richard	1979	C	Guy Lafleur	1988	RW
Frank Mahovlich	1981	LW	Steve Shutt	1993	LW
Yvan Cournoyer	1982	RW	Guy Lapointe	1993	D
Ken Dryden	1983	G	Larry Robinson	1995	D
Jacques Lemaire	1984	C	Scotty Bowman	1991	Coach
Serge Savard	1986	D	Sam Pollock	1978	GM
Jacques Laperrière	1987	D	Jean Béliveau	1972	VP

167 B.   Only two teams

Only two Stanley Cup teams have iced rosters without a future Hall of Fame member on their bench. Both clubs donned the famous blue jerseys and white double-winged wheel crests of the Montreal AAA, winners of the first two Cups, in 1893 and 1894. The most dominant players on the AAA were star forwards Haviland Routh and Billy Barlow. Routh led all goal scorers in the Amateur Hockey Association of Canada's five-team circuit during 1892–93, scoring his league-high 12th goal in the season's final game, a 2–1 win against the Montreal Crystals. The victory edged Ottawa out of first place and automatically awarded the AAA the AHAC crown and, with that title, the inaugural Stanley Cup. The following season, 1893–94, the Cup's maiden postseason, Barlow scored twice in each of two playoff matches—including Game 1's winner against the Montreal Victorias and Game 2's Cup clincher against Ottawa—to become the first hero of Lord Stanley's bowl. Since then, in 120 years of Cup champions, every winning club with Hall-eligible players has sported a Hall of Famer.

Montreal AAA, 1894

168 C. Pat Quinn

The coaching careers of Builders like Pat Quinn are never measured solely in wins or championships. Their success is often more about drive and determination and their relationships with players, though what they win or nearly win does matter, too. Quinn was a journeyman enforcer of 606 NHL games, with nothing radar-worthy except a bone-crushing hit on Bobby Orr that had Bruins fans famously baying, "We want Quinn!" After that though, through three decades, he coached and managed at multiple levels and notched two Jack Adams Awards as top NHL coach and a gold medal for Canada at the 2002 Winter Olympics. Now, the interesting stuff. The cigar-chomping Quinn was an old-school, tough-but-fair bench boss who every player played their hearts out for. As proof, he rightly owns the NHL's record 35-game unbeaten streak with Philadelphia in 1979–80. His Flyers refused to lose for him through 12 weeks, racking up 25 wins and 10 ties—the longest run among the top four major sports leagues. He coached four of his five teams to the playoffs, missing the postseason just five times in 20 years. But without a Stanley Cup, he owns the Cup-less playoff record: 183 games. No coach in league history reached such depths of championship futility, including active bench bosses like Alain Vigneault. Quinn went twice to the final with underdog teams, the Flyers in 1980 and Vancouver in 1994. Quinn knew hockey. "Every press conference with Pat was almost like a tutorial," one reporter said. That kind of knowledge transfer is another measure of Quinn, one that made him a Hall Builder.

169 Scotty Bowman is the most successful Builder in the Hall, having won nine Stanley Cups as a coach and another four in executive positions. After Bowman, which Builder has his name most often on the Cup?

A.
James D. Norris

B.
Jim Devellano

C.
Sam Pollock

D.
Frank Selke

170 What is the most Cups won by an individual on the most teams in the fewest number of years?

A. Four Cups on one team in four years

B. Five Cups on one team in five years

C. Five Cups on two teams in six years

D. Five Cups on three teams in seven years

171 Who is the only individual to claim the Stanley Cup as an NHL player, coach and general manager?

A.
Art Ross

B.
Glen Sather

C.
Jack Adams

D.
Bob Gainey

172 Which pair of Hall of Fame members set the following opposite Stanley Cup records?

- The first is the player who registered the fewest regular-season and playoff games before going on to win the Cup, and the second is the player who registered the highest game totals before claiming the Cup.

A.
Toe Blake and Ed Belfour

B.
Jacques Plante and Ray Bourque

C.
Ken Dryden and Lanny McDonald

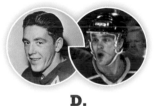

D.
Marcel Pronovost and Luc Robitaille

169 C. Sam Pollock

A man of quiet grace in a brutal game, Sam Pollock was shrewd, calculating, opportunistic and such a brilliant assessor of hockey talent that during his 14-year tenure as Montreal's general manager, the Canadiens won nine Stanley Cups. His name is on the Cup with the Habs another three times for performing different administrative functions, giving him a total of 12 championships and making him the most successful Builder after Scotty Bowman. However, Pollock's triumphs were often criticized, based on the belief that his dynasty teams came gift-wrapped. Pollock countered that chance played no part in drafting Guy Lafleur, Rod Langway or Bob Gainey. "We scouted them, we assessed them. That's not luck. That's hard work." He entered the Hall in 1978 and retired from hockey the next year, the game's best evaluator of player skill working in an NHL club's front office.

Most Stanley Cups by Hall of Fame Builders

Builder	Induction Year	Cup Record
Scotty Bowman	1991	14 (Montreal, 1973, 1976–1979; Pittsburgh, 1991, 1992; Detroit, 1997, 1998, 2002, 2008; Chicago, 2010, 2013, 2015)
Sam Pollock	1978	12 (Montreal, 1959, 1960, 1965, 1966, 1968, 1969, 1971, 1973, 1976–1979)
Frank Selke	1960	9 (Toronto, 1932, 1942, 1945; Montreal, 1953, 1956–1960)
Conn Smythe	1958	8 (Toronto, 1932, 1942, 1945, 1947–1949, 1951, 1962)
Al Arbour*	1996	8 (Detroit, 1954; Chicago, 1961; Toronto, 1962, 1964; NY Islanders, 1980–1983)

*Arbour's first four Cups won as a player.

170 D. Five Cups on three teams in seven years

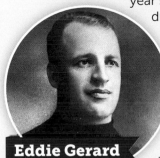

Eddie Gerard

Some individuals may have won more Cups, strung together more consecutive Cups or picked up Cups on more teams, but no one matches Eddie Gerard's record of five championships on three different teams in a seven-year span. Gerard was a career Ottawa Senator during the NHL's formative years. He played forward early on but was moved to defense and paired with George Boucher, where the tandem jelled into one of the most formidable defensive duos in the league. Boucher played the rushing puckhandler and Gerard the gritty rearguard whose intelligence and leadership skills equaled his ability to outmuscle any opponent from the puck. He could always be counted on to score timely goals. Between 1920 and 1926, Gerard captained Ottawa to three Cups, earned another title while playing on loan to Toronto as an emergency fill-in and had his name etched on the Cup a fifth time coaching the Montreal Maroons. He was an original member of the Hall of Fame, inducted in 1945.

Captain Eddie Gerard's Historic Cup Run

Championship Year	Finalists	Gerard's Highlights
1920	Ottawa beat Seattle 3–2 in best-of-five series	Scored 2-1-3 in five games, inspiring end-to-end rush goal in final victory.
1921	Ottawa beat Vancouver 3–2 in best-of-five series	Incurred 44 penalty minutes; assessed match penalty for fighting in final win.
1922	Toronto beat Vancouver 3–2 in best-of-five series	Shut down Vancouver's attack so effectively as a replacement (for injured Harry Cameron) in Game 4, St. Pats won 6–0 and Vancouver refused to let Gerard play for Toronto in Game 5.
1923	Ottawa beat Edmonton 2–0 in best-of-three series	Battled through dislocated shoulder and cut foot; scored once in seven games.
1926	Montreal beat Victoria 3–1 in best-of-five series	Coached Maroons to 20-11-5 record and the Stanley Cup in second year of franchise.

171 C. Jack Adams

Jack Adams was the face of the Detroit Red Wings for almost 35 years. He ushered in the talents of Gordie Howe, Ted Lindsay and Terry Sawchuk while holding down multiple jobs, as coach, general manager, publicist and even traveling secretary. During his Motor City reign he won seven Stanley Cups between 1927 and 1962. But for all he did to build the Detroit franchise from expansion team to champion, it was his seven-year playing career that determined his Hall status—he was inducted as a Player. Adams holds what might be hockey's rarest triple crown: winning the Cup as a player, with Toronto in 1918 and Ottawa in 1927; winning the Cup as a coach, with Detroit in 1936, 1937 and 1943; and winning the Cup as a GM, with Detroit in 1950, 1952, 1954 and 1955. Adams is considered the first NHLer who was successful both as a player and an executive—a Cup winner in each of the NHL's first five decades.

172 B. Jacques Plante and Ray Bourque

Players have been known to make their only NHL appearance during the playoffs for a Stanley Cup winner, but none in that lucky group (Gord Haidy, Doug McKay and Chris Hayes) have been voted into the Hall. Among honored members, rookie Jacques Plante netted the fastest Cup, backstopping Montreal just three times during 1952–53, to replace starter Gerry McNeil, and then playing another four games in the postseason. His 3–0 victory against Chicago in the must-win Game 6 of the semifinal evened the series for the Canadiens. Montreal won Game 7 with Plante in net and went on to defeat Boston in the final, as Plante started two more contests before McNeil returned to lock up the title. Ray Bourque waited the longest for Cup glory. In 22 seasons he missed the playoffs only once and twice went to the final with Boston. However, Bourque didn't become a champion until his last try, with Colorado in 2001. It was his 1,826th game.

Fewest NHL Games to Win a Stanley Cup by a Hall of Famer

Player	Induction Year	1st Cup Team	Regular-Season Games	Playoff Games	Total
Jacques Plante	1978	Montreal, 1953	3	4	7
Toe Blake	1966	Mtl. Maroons, 1935	8	1	9
Marcel Pronovost	1978	Detroit, 1950	0	9	9
Jack Adams	1959	Toronto, 1918	8	2	10

Most NHL Games to Win a Stanley Cup by a Hall of Famer

Player	Induction Year	1st Cup Team	Regular-Season Games	Playoff Games	Total
Ray Bourque	2004	Colorado, 2001	1612	214	1826
Luc Robitaille	2009	Detroit, 2002	1205	155	1360
Lanny McDonald	1992	Calgary, 1989	1111	117	1228
Steve Yzerman	2009	Detroit, 1997	1023	113	1136

Cup Hunters

● ●

The list of Hall of Fame members with Stanley Cups on multiple teams is short. At the very top sits four-team Cup winners Jack Marshall and Hap Holmes, inductees of 1965 and 1972, respectively. Below Marshall and Holmes, the triple-team Cup echelon is reserved for Player honorees Jack Walker, Frank Foyston, Al Arbour and power forward Joe Nieuwendyk, a champion with Calgary, Dallas and New Jersey. In this game, match the players and their championship years on multiple clubs.

For solutions, turn the page.

Part 1

1.	Brett Hull	A. 1986, 1993, 1996, 2001
2.	Glenn Anderson	B. 1986, 2002, 2008
3.	Bryan Trottier	C. 1999, 2002
4.	Patrick Roy	D. 1934, 1940
5.	Art Coulter	E. 1980, 1981, 1982, 1983, 1991, 1992
6.	Chris Chelios	F. 1984, 1985, 1987, 1988, 1990, 1994

Part 2

1.	Scott Niedermayer	A. 1989, 1999, 2003
2.	Joe Mullen	B. 1995, 2000, 2003, 2007
3.	Paul Coffey	C. 1962, 1963, 1964, 1967, 1971, 1973
4.	Frank Mahovlich	D. 1984, 1985, 1987, 1991
5.	Joe Nieuwendyk	E. 1984, 1985, 1987, 1988, 1990, 1994
6.	Mark Messier	F. 1989, 1991, 1992

Cup Hunters

Solutions

Part 1

Player	Championships
1. Brett Hull	C. 1999 Dallas; 2002 Detroit
2. Glenn Anderson	F. 1984, 1985, 1987, 1988, 1990 Edmonton; 1994 NY Rangers
3 Bryan Trottier	E. 1980, 1981, 1982, 1983 NY Islanders; 1991, 1992 Pittsburgh
4. Patrick Roy	A. 1986, 1993 Montreal; 1996, 2001 Colorado
5. Art Coulter	D. 1934 Chicago; 1940 NY Rangers
6. Chris Chelios	B. 1986 Montreal; 2002, 2008 Detroit

Part 2

Player	Championships
1. Scott Niedermayer	B. 1995, 2000, 2003 New Jersey; 2007 Anaheim
2. Joe Mullen	F. 1989 Calgary; 1991, 1992 Pittsburgh
3. Paul Coffey	D. 1984, 1985, 1987 Edmonton; 1991 Pittsburgh
4. Frank Mahovlich	C. 1962, 1963, 1964, 1967 Toronto; 1971, 1973 Montreal
5. Joe Nieuwendyk	A. 1989 Calgary; 1999 Dallas; 2003 New Jersey
6. Mark Messier	E. 1984, 1985, 1987, 1988, 1990 Edmonton; 1994 NY Rangers

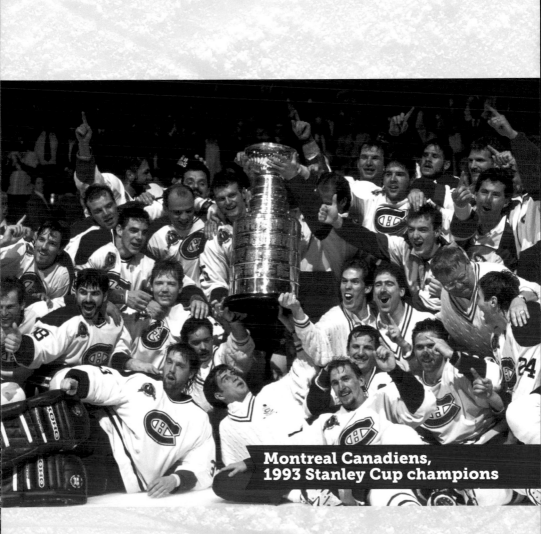

**Montreal Canadiens,
1993 Stanley Cup champions**

Acknowledgments

Thanks to the following organizations for use of quoted and/or statistical material:

The Hockey News (various issues).

The National Hockey League Official Guide and Record Book (various editions), Total Hockey and Total NHL, published by Dan Diamond & Associates.

The IIHF Guide and Record Book 2013, published by Fenn/McClelland & Stewart.

How Hockey Happened by J.W. (Bill) Fitsell, published by Quarry Press Inc.

Thanks also to the Associated Press, Canadian Press, Chicago Tribune, Edmonton Journal, Elias Sports Bureau, The Globe and Mail, Hockey Night in Canada, Detroit Free Press, Montreal Gazette, National Post, New York Times, Ottawa Journal, Toronto Star and Sports Illustrated.

Thanks as well to the publishers of numerous other books and publications, including Honoured Members by the Hockey Hall of Fame; The Meaning of Puck and The Stick by Bruce Dowbiggin; Players and Lord Stanley's Cup by Andrew Podnieks; Hockey Hall of Fame Book of Goalies, edited by Steve Cameron; Canada's Game, edited by Andrew C. Holman; The Trail of the Stanley Cup by Charles L. Coleman; The Rules of Hockey by James Duplacey; Cold War by Roy MacSkimming; 1972 — The Summit Series: Canada vs. USSR, Stats, Lies & Videotape, The UNTOLD Story of Hockey's Series of the Century by Richard J. Bendell; and Now Is the Winter, edited by Jamie Dopp and Richard Harrison.

Also helpful in the research were Internet databases such as nhl.com, hhof.com, iihf.com, hockey-reference.com, quanthockey.com, hockeydraftcentral.com, hockeygoalies.org, nhlofficials.com, insidehockey.com, espn.com, hockeydb.com, hockeyfights.com and sihrhockey.org.

The author gratefully acknowledges all the support from Phil Pritchard and Craig Campbell at the Hockey Hall of Fame; Ralph Dinger and Benny Ercolani of the NHL; Jean-Patrice Martel at the Society for International Hockey Research; McLennan Library staff at McGill University; Steve Cameron, Julie Takasaki and Lionel Koffler at Firefly Books; the many hockey writers and broadcast and web journalists who have made the game better through their own work; fact-checker Richard J. Bendell and proofreader Kerry Banks for key saves throughout this second edition; and designer Gareth Lind and copyeditor Ronnie Shuker for their dedication and expertise.

Index of
Trivia Answers

Index

Index